Kara Martin's latest contribution to the global faith-at-work movement is practical, personal, and passionate. Page after page is filled with tried and tested ideas that will appeal to readers who want to integrate their faith and their work. There is a raw honesty in the book — no glib triumphalism here — as Kara draws on the daily reality of her own and others' experiences, then brings biblical wisdom to bear providing deeper insight. Having worked with Kara on a number of work and faith projects in recent years, it is no surprise that her passion for the gospel impact in the workplace is evident throughout. If you are a church leader, please read this book and be equipped and encouraged with the many easily implemented tools provided. If you are a Christian in the workplace, get a copy — read, mark, and inwardly digest!

Murray Wright, Founding Director, Malyon Workplace, Malyon College

We need this book. We need it because we want to have welcoming workplaces shaped by the heart of God. We need it because we aspire to be leaders who serve with the character of Jesus. We need it because we endeavour to have beautiful work spaces inspired by the Spirit of God. I also need this book. I need it because it gives a clear window into the questions asked by the congregation I serve. I need it because it helps me understand the questions I ask about my own role and calling. I need it because it directs me towards life lived in the kingdom of God through practical and tangible means. I need it because I haven't come across anything like it in its depth of wisdom, breadth of experience, ease of accessibility, and writing shaped by the character of Jesus.

Graeme Anderson, Senior Pastor Northside Baptist Church, Author of Follow: Experiencing Life with Jesus, *Adjunct Lecturer, Spiritual Formation, Morling College*

D1570811

Unfortunately, throughout the centuries, there has been little engagement by theologians with the ways God empowers Christians for their ordinary work lives. Kara Martin's work fills a very deep void where Christian discipleship and spiritual formation material for the workplace **should be** in our libraries and Christian bookshops. The practical studies provided in *Workship 2* allow application to the gritty, tangible aspects of life in the real world. I can't wait to redesign our Hillsong College Christian spirituality course with these volumes!

Tanya Riches, Researcher, Senior Lecturer,
Masters Program Coordinator, Songwriter

Kara Martin has done it again! Often with movies, music albums, or books, the second or sequel is a fizzer. *Workship 2: How to Flourish at Work* is no fizzer. It has the same characteristic savvy use of Scripture, rootedness in real life, strong biblical relational framework and emphasis, up-to-date statistics, and stories. The 20+ short chapters have a similar holistic structure: a pertinent workplace issue, outline of a biblical and Christian approach, thoughtful questions for groups or individuals, reflective prayers and added resources to go on with. However, many of the chapter subjects are rarely dealt with in the faith and work literature: hospitality and work, beauty at work, women and work, the future of work. It scratches where workers itch, gives them voice, and equips pastors to equip them. It's a recipe for a really rich and flourishing working life and for churches that will flourish as their people do in their work.

Gordon Preece, Author, Editor of five books on work, Board Member of the
Theology of Work Project, a Leader of Lausanne Marketplace Ministry,
Pastor and Ethicist

Workship 2 is a page-turner, filled with vivid storytelling and biblical reflections rich and deep in what it means to do kingdom work in everyday workplaces. From celebrating beauty in our work, to learning the unforced rhythms of grace as an antidote to workplace stress, to bringing your church to work, this hand-in-glove companion to *Workship 1* is a treasure trove of practical wisdom anchored in Jesus, "the irresistible leader". Kara Martin has written an indispensable resource for the everyday worker, for the one who encourages other workplace Christians and for those who train church leaders.

Rosemary Wong, Consultant Endocrinologist, Chair of Melbourne School of Theology, Vice-Chair of Eastern College Australia, Chair Christian Medical and Dental Fellowship of Australia (Vic)

In *Workship 2: How to Flourish at Work*, Kara Martin provides helpful and practical perspectives on how work and worship can be integrated in the workplace. This new book extends our understanding that work and life are gifts from God and they are both acts of worship. She challenged me to think more deeply and creatively on how to lead in humility and service to others. Kara also explores the ways that churches can respond, encourage and develop workplace Christians. It is refreshing to consider how churches can equip us to engage more fully in the workplace with the awareness of God's presence. The barriers in our minds dividing secular and sacred work can be broken down. How fulfilling it is to live our whole lives for Christ!

Jeannie Trudel, President, Christian Heritage College, Queensland

Workship 2 is a welcome combination of theology, practice, prayer, and reflection. Many Christians struggle with what it means to see their places of work as places of ministry. It's not just using the workplace as a springboard for evangelism; it is seeing the workplace as an environment in which we can show Christian hospitality, ethics, and creative beauty. Some jobs lend themselves more easily to being seen as places of ministry, but any legitimate work can be God-honouring. Last week a man who crashes cars for a living (to test safety ratings) asked me about what it would look like to worship God through his work. Having now read *Workship 2*, I feel better equipped to answer the question. This book gives many practical applications for how to bridge the Sunday to Monday divide.

Ian Smith, Principal, Christ College Sydney

Kara Martin's book *Workship Volume 2: How to Flourish at Work* is a wonderful extension to her first book, *Workship: How to Use Your Work to Worship God.* This topic is very close to my heart as a nursing facilitator and in my involvement teaching spiritual care in a nursing context to many audiences around the world. Kara is committed to helping us bridge the gap between our Sunday faith and our Monday chaos. I appreciate her rich biblical foundations and then the counter-balance offering real ideas, encouragement, and motivation to flourish at work and to be change agents with depth, purpose, and love. It is a powerful book and relevant to those who truly desire to infuse work and worship in a dynamic and rich way.

Gabrielle Macauley, Clinical Facilitator in Nursing, and President, Nurses Christian Fellowship Australia

In *Workship*, Kara Martin helped us see that our work, however noticed or hidden, matters to God and to the world. In this follow up volume, she gets even more practical, showing us how to bring beauty and hospitality into the workplace, deal with organisational stress and co-worker conflict, navigate tricky ethical dilemmas, and more. Here is your go-to manual for making the workdays meaningful.

Sheridan Voysey, Writer, Speaker, Broadcaster, and Author of Resilient: Your Invitation to a Jesus-Shaped Life, *and* Resurrection Year: Turning Broken Dreams into New Beginnings

Kara Martin has provided the whole church with much needed wisdom here. We can no longer just encourage one another to "make a difference" at work. We need wisdom to know how to do that in the midst of the multiple challenges that we face. And pastors need her practical wisdom to know how to really help their workers. This volume is a gift for those of us who believe that all in Christ have a vocation and that it is the task of the whole church to enable us to live out the implications of the whole gospel in our whole lives.

Neil Hudson, Director, Church Relationships,
London Institute for Contemporary Christianity

This short book is helpful both for workplace Christians seeking to show forth God's kingdom through their work, and churches hoping to resource them. Real-life case studies and survey information, Scripture study, theological probing, prayers, and application questions all guide the reader into a deeper understanding of the challenges and joys of being a Christian at work.

Jennifer Woodruff Tait, Editor, The Green Room *blog*

Workship 2 is not another tick-and-flick guide from which a few key phrases and reflective activities lingered on my mind before being quickly filed away on the 'read' bookshelf. Instead, Kara Martin has brought together a plethora of resources with strong representation from Australian authors, case studies, research and legislation — rare in the "Christians at work" movement which I observe to be dominated by North American male writers and paid urban contexts. It will help Christians — young and old — and church leaders integrate God's intention for work into discussion, teaching, and practice. I devoured this book, from the first paragraph which elicited one of several "Amen sister!" moments, to the brief cameo of 90s band, Nirvana.

Clare, Ordinary Worker

Workship 2

How to Flourish at Work

Kara Martin

Workship 2

How to Flourish at Work

Kara Martin

Published by
Graceworks Private Limited
22 Sin Ming Lane
#04-76 Midview City
Singapore 573969
www.graceworks.com.sg

ISBN: 978-981-11-7234-2

A CIP record for this book is available from the National Library Board, Singapore.

1 2 3 4 5 6 7 8 9 10 • 26 25 24 23 22 21 20 19 18 17

Contents

Foreword

My journey of discovering that my work is an act of worship to God has spanned the last 10 years. Over that time, I have read almost every title on being a Christian in business. So, I am delighted to be asked to write the foreword to the latest and most helpful book on bringing faith into the everyday aspects of our work.

Kara Martin's book *Workship 2* is a guide to awaken and equip us for the roles where many of us spend much of our time and effort. I first met Kara when she was working at Ridley College's Marketplace Institute. Since then, we have collaborated on a range of projects in the area of faith and work, and I have always valued Kara's practical insights on seeing our work from God's perspective.

I have had the amazing privilege of working in a number of senior leadership roles in the technology and government sectors across the Asia Pacific, from Singapore, Kuala Lumpur, Hong Kong, to Taipei, Manila, Bangkok, Phnom Penh, Jakarta, to Sydney, Melbourne, and Auckland. I find it fascinating to compare how people in these different cities work, lead, create businesses, products, or services, and what they will do to obtain fulfilment from work.

From my observations, there is one thing these cities have in common. Not only does work occupy a large part of people's lives, but also it is becoming more complex and increasingly how people define themselves.

Workers are hungry for career guidance and advice on issues such as working with difficult people, navigating ethical challenges, handling stress, and balancing the demands of work with family. I have heard these questions asked by both women and men from every cultural, language, and income group.

I am convinced there is a deep human desire in each of us to understand, *"What is the true purpose of our work?"* While there are numerous books to help us discover our purpose, we are still left with the real-world challenges of integrating our faith with everyday work.

So here is the good news… the wait is over!

Many of us appreciate practical wisdom, so when I read Kara Martin's *Workship 2*, I knew I had found just the tool. Baby boomers are often asked to mentor the next generation of leaders, yet they struggle to find practical and accessible tools to use with their mentorees. Many Gen Xers and Gen Ys crave the sense of being valued and equipped which come from being mentored. But often they don't know how to approach a mentor or frame the deeper questions on faith and work.

From Singapore to Shanghai, from Manila to Melbourne, people are wrestling with questions like: How do I do my work God's way? How do I bring his purposes alive by my work? Is there a biblical framework for how I decide how to work? Each chapter of *Workship 2* lays out these deeper issues in a simple accessible way and concludes with probing questions and a relevant prayer.

Like iron sharpening iron, Kara challenges our thinking with these contrasts — gospel work vs. secular work, ministry vs. other work, eternal work vs. temporal work. Both volumes of *Workship* use as foundation a radical yet liberating claim "that our work is actually God's work." Any consideration or understanding of our work and career will be incomplete if done in isolation from God.

Workship 2 also brings fresh, insightful, and biblical affirmations into the highly volatile issue of how women and men can work alongside each other in ways that both can flourish. Workers in both secular and Christian organisations will find that this chapter equips them to have meaningful marketplace discussions on such a vital societal issue.

No thoughtful book on faith and work can end without providing a biblical framework for processing the experience of unemployment, and for looking at the future of work and the changes that will likely affect people. Kara provides ways to examine and respond to these issues at the personal, structural, and Christian community levels.

Whatever your work, wherever you live, however long you intend to work, there is wisdom in every chapter. I commend this book to you. Mentors and mentorees, small group leaders, student Christian groups, book clubs, senior ministers and ministry teams, and leaders of faith-based organisations — grab some friends or colleagues and read it together. Your perspective on work will be transformed.

Wendy Simpson OAM is the executive chair of Wengeo Group, a private investment company based in Sydney, Australia. She was formerly the Senior Vice President for Alcatel Asia Pacific based in Shanghai, and the North Asian Trade Commissioner for the Victorian Government, based in China. She is Board Member of World Vision Australia, the first female recipient of the Ridley College Faith and Work Award, and has been inducted into the Australian Businesswomen's Hall of Fame.

A Prayer for Work

Lord,
I will always be disappointed at work —
by the perceived defects and inadequacies of my colleagues,
by inefficient systems,
by corporate and individual failure to live up to projected ideals,
and by my own failings.
I will always be disappointed
unless I look to you.

Unless I look to you for purpose and know you as
my source of inspiration and energy,
I will not last.
You alone can be my reason,
pure and unending; to persevere,
to keep giving of myself,
to keep responding to failures of ideals with kindness and patience.

Unless I see my work as **your** work
I will grow conceited or disheartened.
Unless I recognise that
you, with great grace, are allowing me to participate in your work,
work will become an idol or something I resent.

Unless I keep stepping back and viewing work in the context of
your good plan
I risk distraction and distortion.
I risk losing sight of your hands
shaping and moulding all things for your purposes.

Lord, I cannot do any of these things myself.
I do not have the memory or the perspective
To cleave to you always through my working.
I want to see my work through your eyes,
through the lens of your plan.
With joy!
You will have to make this happen.
Please Lord, work so in me to remember all these things.
To be your hands and feet
And to walk in step with you always.

Imogen Herperger
(Imogen wrote this poem–prayer after reading Workship *Volume 1)*

Introduction

In April 2017, in a beautiful café on magnificent church grounds in the heart of Singapore, I launched the first volume of *Workship*.

It was a surreal experience. Dr Clive Lim, himself an entrepreneur and Regent College lecturer, spoke warmly about my book. His daughter, a famous model, was the first person to ask me to sign her copy of my book. My response was to laugh awkwardly as I had never expected to be asked.

Since then, I have grown accustomed to the experience of being an author. But I have never gotten used to the way God has used the book and in his grace allowed me insights as to its impact.

I received a text from Angela, an administrator in a hospital:

I feel I've been given a voice. To be acknowledged that working is important and not second class to full-time mission. At my previous church, I was made to feel guilty for working full time, but we workers were still required to support the 'real' work of those in full-time church work. I feel heard and appreciated and worthwhile.

Later she wrote:

Mission month at my church is coming up in June but *just* those first two chapters give mission month a *whole* new meaning!

It's not just about those in full-time overseas mission work — it needs to include me! The humble pen pusher with a different view of my day-to-day mission on the ground at the hospital, for crying out loud!!! Me!

Clare came along to my Brisbane book launch with her copy of the book, already purchased, read, highlighted, underlined, and with notes scribbled on nearly every page. She had first connected with me on my *Workship* Facebook page where she wrote:

> A wonderful, wonderful piece of work, *Workship*. Have prayers, commitments, and snippets from the book posted around the home and office computer screen! Looking forward to Volume 2 — buy Volume 1, people, buy!

Since we made contact, Clare has used her work at a university to help research the future of work chapter in this volume.

Yenny from an Indonesian Bible study group, who evidently knew my book better than I, asked me if I had failed to make the point that God made us to work? I had not been explicit about that point, and I agreed that the evidence from Genesis was that God had made us in the image of himself, a working God, and given us the command of working to care for his creation.

Patrick told me about the difference it had made thinking of work as a place where people can express their worship of God.

> Usually people think of the church as the only place they can do work for God, but the idea of *Workship* helps people think about their work in a different way. It too can be a place where you can worship God.

While these stories are encouraging, I am conscious that a book alone is not going to change the situation for Angela, Clare, Yenny, and Patrick in the long term. What they need are churches that are supporting, encouraging, and equipping them for their everyday work.

They need affirmation and application ideas, and a sense of being part of a community that is doing God's work in the everyday.

They also need more examples of what it means to see work as **kingdom work** — to face the challenges of everyday workplaces, and to see the opportunities for giving colleagues and customers a sniff of the fragrance of Christ through their ordinary work.

I never felt this more acutely than when I was running a meeting with a guest speaker, Trish, the Australian leader of a large overseas organisation. She had just explained how hard she focuses on her decision-making, to make decisions that reflect the character of Jesus. She told us how she spends significant time praying through her daily routine.

She described how close she feels to God when she is in a boardroom, how she feels God's presence as she relies totally on him. She had told us of recent spiritual conversations as people wondered why she was different.

She asked for questions, and someone asked: "What are you doing for your local church?"

I had to interrupt and explain that we were listening to someone who saw her daily work as her place of ministry. My guest graciously replied that she travels two Sundays a month, so being part of regular rosters is very difficult. She said that she recently had a conversation with her pastor to explain her lack of attendance and the nature of the work she did.

The questioner was unperturbed: "But surely you could give a talk, or use your leadership skills. The church could use you."

My guest admitted that she helped out at the coffee cart when she could, which seemed to somewhat appease her audience.

I bit my tongue, but this precisely illustrates my great frustration. The church's function is to equip its people to do God's work. Rather than being a place where my guest felt guilty for not giving more, it should be a place of refuge, nurture, teaching, and prayer that empowers her to be Christ's light in otherwise dark places. It should be the place where she gathers with others to celebrate God, and is then sent out as the church scattered to work for his glory.

The questioner should have asked: "What is your church doing for you, to support the great work you are doing for God?"

So, I humbly present Volume 2.

Section 1 includes practical wisdom for the workplace: positive ideas for making a difference, and helpful suggestions for how to respond to common issues.

Section 2 provides information for churches about responding to the needs of workplace Christians in their congregations. There are ideas for equipping activities within church services, within church communities, and beyond the church walls.

I want to thank the churches, Bible study groups, media outlets, colleges, and conference organisers who have asked me to participate in their services, meetings, podcasts and programs to speak about how we can *workship*. Some of what we explored together is included in this volume. May God use it to his glory, to increase his kingdom and to bless his earth.

Introduction to Section 1:
Practical Wisdom for Working

Volume 1 of *Workship* established a sound biblical basis for understanding God's view of work, and how the gospel can be expressed through workers who are Christians, in their working and in their workplace via the spiritual disciplines. It also examined some core concepts for all Christians in thinking about their work and their organisations:

- Vocation
- Work and identity
- Working relationships
- Kingdom business

In Volume 2 of *Workship*, I have collated more practical wisdom for your daily working.

There are positive ideas for making a difference in the workplace:

- Hospitality at work
- Jesus-shaped leadership
- Beauty in the workplace

There are helpful suggestions for responding to common issues:

- Ethical decision-making
- Dealing with stress
- Work-life balance
- Handling bullying and conflict
- Toxic workplaces

- Non-selfish ambition
- A biblical reflection on unemployment

There are ideas for new areas of Christian thinking:

- Women and work
- The future of work

These are some of the issues most often raised at speaking engagements and mentoring sessions. I cannot pretend to deliver a complete answer to each of these issues, but I hope to point you to some biblical concepts and practical ideas that will help you make a difference as a Christian in your workplace.

Chapter 1

Hospitality and Work

(Portions of this chapter appeared in an article on the website Life@
Work, *hosted by City Bible Forum, Melbourne[1])*

When I started at my new job I was a little surprised by how unfriendly
it was. People sat in their cubicles and seemed to avoid each other. If I
stopped to say hello, sometimes they wouldn't even look up. There was
no sharing or offers of help. People seemed to prefer avoiding "hello"
in the morning and "goodbye" at the end of the day. Sometimes, I was
surprised to discover I was the last person left in the building.

This led to an atmosphere that was the antithesis of hospitality.
Hospitality is the generous welcoming of guests or strangers. It is about
creating a safe and friendly place to build relationships and do work.

It is also something I see as foundational to being a Christian.
Even in the ancient world providing hospitality was considered an
obligation. The Greeks made it a virtue, but Christians added a new
element, *koinonia* — the provision of fellowship.

Our God Provides Hospitality
Our God is hospitable: he creates and provides everything we need
in abundance. Even when we reject him, he continues to reach out in
love. In the Old Testament, he provides specific commands to welcome
the stranger and foreigner, and provide for them. In Deuteronomy
10:18–19 he says, "He defends the cause of the fatherless and the
widow, and loves the foreigner residing among you, giving them
food and clothing. And you are to love those who are foreigners, for
you yourselves were foreigners in Egypt." The prophets warned the
Israelites of judgement because of their poor treatment of foreigners:
"This is what the LORD says: Do what is just and right. Rescue from the
hand of the oppressor the one who has been robbed. Do no wrong or
violence to the foreigner, the fatherless or the widow, and do not shed
innocent blood in this place" (Jeremiah 22:3).

---

[1] Kara Martin, "Creating a welcoming place at work", *Life@Work*, 7 March 2015. https://lifeatwork.
org.au/content/creating-welcoming-place-work (cited 7-Feb-2018).

Jesus is the ultimate example of God's expression of hospitality. He left a place of comfort, security, and power, to enter our world as a vulnerable baby and a man rejected by all (Philippians 2:5–11). In spite of the way others treated him, Jesus offered food and healing and welcomes all — even those who were ignored or rejected such as children, tax collectors, common sinners, and prostitutes.

God, in his grace offers salvation to all, not wishing anyone to perish. This salvation is a free gift requiring no work or effort from us, merely assent. It is an offer to enter a hospitable place with God (Ephesians 2:8–10).

So, in offering hospitality we are bearing witness to the character of God, and also giving a glimpse of the coming kingdom. It is also a direct command: "Share with the Lord's people who are in need. Practice hospitality" (Romans 12:13).

For an in-depth examination of biblical material, especially pointers to Jesus' practice of hospitality, see "Hospitality" by Patricia Kerr in *The Complete Book of Everyday Christianity*.[2]

Practising Hospitality in the Workplace

I decided that I would try and make small changes in my workplace:

- I kept my door open so that I could see and hear when people walked by, and I called out to them when they do.
- Whenever people paused by my door, I would invite them in and ask them to be seated.
- I made my office fun with coffee poetry magnets, posters, and interesting objects.
- I had laughter if they had something fun to share and tissues if they felt sad.
- I shared chocolate.
- If I went out for coffee I asked if anyone else would like one.

---

[2] Robert Banks and R. Paul Stevens (Eds.), *The Complete Book of Everyday Christianity* (Singapore: Graceworks, 2011).

- When I was leaving for the day, I went around and said goodbye.
- I invited people to lunch for one-on-one conversations, or for drinks when there was something to celebrate.

After a while, I noticed changes at my workplace. People tended to stop by and chat. No one left without saying goodbye to me. I made good use of the tissue box as people shared hard things. I enjoyed many laughs. People came in to share important life-stage news with me: engagements, wedding arrangements, and pregnancies.

The German word for hospitality is *Gastfreundschaft*, which means "friendship for the guest". In my small efforts to befriend others, I hope that I had helped people make a move from being strangers to friends with the God whom I serve, to Jesus who is my inspiration, empowered by the Spirit to serve.

More Examples in the Workplace

Some of my work has been with the Christian Medical and Dental Fellowship of Australia, and I have noted that several of their biggest breakthroughs in reaching colleagues is through providing hospitality.

Alex told me about the time he and other fellowship colleagues bought a huge basket of hot cross buns and left it in the hospital staffroom with a note explaining it was a gift for Easter from the CMDFA.

The group had more feedback and questions from this simple act than any other event or activity.

Food is naturally linked to hospitality and can be used effectively. Everyone in the office will know when you have baked something, hosted a birthday celebration, or shouted a round of coffees.

City Bible Forum in Melbourne ran an effective outreach activity where members were encouraged to invite a work colleague to lunch. The free lunch initiative was a way of showing hospitality and developing deeper relationships.

The Potential of Hospitality

Henri Nouwen is much more eloquent than I:

> Hospitality is not to change people but to offer them space where change can take place. It is not to bring men and women over to our side, but to offer freedom not disturbed by dividing lines. It is not to lead our neighbour to a corner where there are no alternatives left, but to open a wide spectrum of options for choice and commitment. It is not an educated intimidation with good books, good stories, and good works, but the liberation of fearful hearts so that words can find roots and bear ample fruit.[3]

---

[3] Henri Nouwen, *Reaching Out: The Three Movements of the Spiritual Life* (New York: Doubleday, 1986), 71–72.

Prayer:

Dear Lord,

Thank you for teaching us what hospitality is.

Thank you that even when we were strangers, you welcomed us as friends. Thank you that you provide a welcome place for us.

Help us to make our workplaces hospitable.

Challenge us to be creative and generous in what we do to make others feel welcome, in creating a friendly place.

Thank you for the inspiration you give us in terms of creativity and generosity.

Protect us from self-interest, pride, or ambition that might stop us from being more hospitable.

Teach us to honour you.

AMEN

Taking It Further:

1

How hospitable is your workplace? Where are the places that you could make a difference, starting with your immediate work area?

2

How can you initiate intentional acts of hospitality? Could you bake? Host a celebration? Shout a round of coffees? Take someone out for a free lunch?

3

Flick through the Gospel of Luke, noticing all the different acts of hospitality that Jesus showed. How many of these things could you do? (Feeding, praying for others, taking time to listen, etc.)

4

Read Henri Nouwen's quote and think through the times you have been shown such hospitality. What new ideas are prompted in terms of how you might make your working/workplace more hospitable?

Chapter 2

Jesus-Shaped Leadership

A Tale of Two Leaders

The first story is of a woman who ran a startup digital technology company that grew quickly during boom times but became very vulnerable during the global financial crisis. Her company was doing the best they could to prepare their new product for launch, but it started to become obvious that there were significant issues with the marketplace's appetite for new products during a downturn.

The woman worked long hours and was honest with her employees who all worked hard and innovatively. When it became obvious that their financial backers were pulling out, she tried hard to secure another buyer. Throughout everything she kept everyone informed.

Finally, the buyer pulled out and the money ran out. She notified everyone that the next day would be their last with the organisation. At that point she had a long discussion with God in prayer. What had happened to all the good work they had done? Why had God not blessed them? She had tried to be faithful in her working, why was that not enough?

When the employees met together the next day, she told them the most recent developments and what would happen next. She would be organising to sell off remaining assets and their intellectual property, and continuing to do her best to ensure the product they all believed in would make it to market.

She thanked them for their work and celebrated their achievements. When she finished, she received a standing ovation which brought her to tears. At that point she realised there was still value in all the work that had been done — the relationships that had been formed, and the creative culture she had worked and prayed to form.

The second story is about a Christian leader in a large bank that underwent a significant restructure. For a couple of months, he and his team were in limbo about what would happen as there was no apparent role for him or his team in the new structure.

Eventually, he called a meeting with his team to make an announcement. "I have bad news and good news," he explained. "The bad news is that there is still a lot of uncertainty about the future. The work we do still needs to be done, but this team will probably be split up, and in all likelihood there will be some redundancies.

"The good news is that the company has found a new role for me, which I will be starting in a couple of weeks' time. After that you will need to continue without a leader for a period."

When he finished there was stunned silence.

The Intimacy of Leadership

Leadership is actually a very intimate relationship, even in a work situation. Leadership requires followership, and followers need to have confidence in the competency of their leaders, and in the care the leader has for them as a team. When this dynamic is working well, there is incredible opportunity for effective working and personal growth. When it goes badly, there is a lot of pain and disappointment, and poor work with the potential for conflict.

Christians have a lot of opportunity and resources to speak into the leadership vacuum in the world. We follow one of the greatest leaders of all time. Jesus was a superlative recruiter, educator, communicator, visionary, strategist, and influencer.

He has also given us the most powerful concept of leadership: being a servant leader, which was entirely counter-cultural at that time, as it often seems today.

We do hear positive stories of leadership when great things are achieved, but frequently the proving ground for leadership is during the difficult times, the setbacks, and the failures.

Jesus: The Irresistible Leader

During my time at Bible College, and following, I have had the privilege of teaching leadership and management to students. When I was first planning the unit with the founding dean of the Marketplace Institute, Dr Ken Barnes, we agreed on one characteristic of Jesus' leadership that most inspired us — he was irresistible. His ideas and behaviour attracted many but threatened those in religious authority and the politically powerful.

The following journey through the Gospel of Matthew describes what Jesus-shaped leadership is like.

First of all, Jesus was born great. His birth was foretold throughout the Old Testament, especially by the prophets. In the birth narrative in Matthew (1:1–2:23), Jesus was anticipated and honoured even though he had a humble birth. He was worshipped right from the start.

Although some of us might be born into family dynasties or groomed for certain leadership roles, all of us will still need to prove our right to lead. Jesus did this through his teaching and miracles, and we likewise must win support through our character, behaviour, wisdom, and gifts.

Matthew 3:1–4:11 describes how Jesus built on the work of others — the prophets and explicitly John the Baptist — and prepared himself for his leadership role. He spent much time working as a village carpenter before entering into his itinerant teaching and disciple-making work. Part of his preparation involved a ritual to recognise his identity: his baptism, followed by a time of prayer and fasting.

We too must be conscious of how we build on the work of those who went before us and those around us. We need deep preparation for leading, but must never think that our leadership skills are sufficient as they are. The world is always changing and there are always new skills to learn. Celebrating the importance of rituals, as well as paying attention to personal internal work, can greatly deepen our experience and expression of leadership.

Matthew 4:12–9:38 demonstrates the irresistible Jesus most clearly as he called disciples and gathered crowds with his powerful teaching and healing. He was engaging and social in his style and message, and in whom he addressed, even outcasts. The crowds recognised his authority and distinctiveness from other religious leaders (Matthew 7:29).

What we do — and how we do it — is noticed by and communicated among onlookers and our followers. There must be consistency between our words and actions. We don't have to try to be like others, but we must find our own authentic style.

In Matthew 10:1–42, Jesus the delegator emerged. He trained up his disciples for their future work. He modelled the behaviour, gave them explicit instructions, then sent them out. In the Luke account, Jesus sent the disciples twice: first the 12 closest disciples, and then the 72 (Luke 9 and 10). Afterwards he debriefed them about their experiences and reinforced key messages.

Jesus demonstrated to us the key aspects of delegation, particularly in giving those we delegate full authority to do their work effectively; and in debriefing the experience to reinforce key messages.

In Matthew 23:8–10, Jesus established himself as the preeminent mentor among human mentors. He described himself as teacher and instructor, as well as the Messiah, the chosen one, and the Saviour.

In the chapter on mentoring in Section 2, we will look in more detail at the importance of mentoring, which we might call discipleship within the church context. Sometimes we miss the importance of the roles of teacher and instructor in our leadership — and only Jesus has the right to be seen as Messiah and Saviour!

In Matthew 26, Jesus pointed to the costs of leadership. For him, it will be the ultimate cost — his life sacrificed. His disciples also paid that heavy cost. For those of us called to be leaders, it will often mean being criticised and attacked, with possible attempts at being overthrown. Many leaders I have known have spent periods when they were weary, confused, frustrated, and wondered if they were doing the right thing.

However, the key to Jesus' leadership is his relationship within the Trinity. He remained in the Father and was fed by the Spirit who was his ally in leading (John 14:26). Christian leaders have the benefit of a close relationship with God through prayer, his Word, and his Spirit, through which we have access to peace in spite of the costs and the trials (John 14:27).

The Two Postures of Jesus
There are two postures of a leader that Jesus introduced to the world. Previously, they would have been the antithesis of what a leader was considered to be.

Humility

The first posture is humility. In the Greco-Roman world into which Jesus was born, the predominant values were receiving honour and boasting of one's achievements. In stark contrast, Jesus taught humility: "The greatest among you will be your servant. For those who exalt themselves will be humbled, and those who humble themselves will be exalted" (Matthew 23:11–12).

More importantly, he *exemplified* humility, commanding others not to boast about what he had done (Mark 1:34, 1:40–44, 7:36, 16:20), letting others name him (John 4:39–42, Luke 22:66–71), and finally, allowing himself to die a humiliating death on a cross (Philippians 2:8).

One of the first hymns[1] of the church celebrates the humility of Jesus — he who left heaven and his rightful place as God, to become human for our sakes, and was obedient even to the point of death on a cross (Philippians 2:6–11).

Paul exhorted all Christians to demonstrate Jesus' character by being humble themselves (Philippians 2:3–5). Early church leaders James and Peter also take up this exhortation: "Humble yourselves before the Lord, and he will lift you up" (James 4:10), and "Humble yourselves, therefore, under God's mighty hand, that he may lift you up in due time" (1 Peter 5:6).[2]

Serving others

The second posture that Jesus demonstrated is servanthood. While humility is an inward-looking virtue, something we cultivate and internalise so that it becomes part of us, serving others is outwardly focused.

Serving was again something that Jesus taught and modelled: "For even the Son of Man did not come to be served, but to serve, and to

---

[1] Philippians 2:6–11 is believed to be the first hymn of the church, a song affirming Jesus' humility in coming to earth and dying for us.

[2] For an extended examination of the Christian gift of humility to the world, read *Humilitas* by John Dickson (Grand Rapids: Zondervan, 2011).

give his life as a ransom for many" (Mark 10:45, which flowed on from his teaching in 9:35).

He also set an example through beautiful acts of service, the most famous being the washing of the disciples' feet at the Last Supper (John 13:1–17): "Now that I, your Lord and Teacher, have washed your feet, you also should wash one another's feet. I have set you an example that you should do as I have done for you."

Finally, his posture of service was again promoted and modelled by the leaders of the early church:

- Paul: "You, my brothers and sisters, were called to be free. But do not use your freedom to indulge the flesh; rather, serve one another humbly in love." (Galatians 5:13)
- John: "This is how we know what love is: Jesus Christ laid down his life for us. And we ought to lay down our lives for our brothers and sisters. If anyone has material possessions and sees a brother or sister in need but has no pity on them, how can the love of God be in that person? Dear children, let us not love with words or speech but with actions and in truth." (1 John 3:16–18)
- Peter: "Each of you should use whatever gift you have received to serve others, as faithful stewards of God's grace in its various forms." (1 Peter 4:10)

The wisdom of these postures is recognised by those who study leadership today. In a famous study by Jim Collins, he examined companies who had moved from 'Good' to 'Great' and defined the determining characteristic of their respective CEOs as Level 5 Leadership. A Level 5 leader "builds enduring greatness through a paradoxical blend of personal humility and professional will." This was not what Collins expected, but he could not ignore the evidence.[3]

In a follow-up study published after the Global Financial Crisis, Collins described the stages of downfall of once great corporations:

---

[3] Jim Collins, *Good to Great* (New York: HarperCollins, 2001). See Chapter 2.

hubris born of success, leading to undisciplined pursuit of more, followed by denial of risk and peril, then grasping for salvation, until final capitulation to irrelevance or death. It is remarkable how many of these stages involve an attitude that is the antithesis of a focus on serving others.[4]

The Humble Leader

The greatest Christian leaders I have known have been unpretentious, humble, focused on others and not themselves, and keen to serve. One time, N.T. Wright ("Just call me Tom") was speaking at our college, and I was invited to lunch with him and another lecturer. I was prepared to sit and just drink in words of wisdom from an author and speaker I admired so much.

However, Tom astounded me when he asked me how I was doing, and really listened to my answer. I had been commuting to work from another state, and we then had an interesting discussion about the concept of home and the importance of geography.

It was a genuine conversation where he was more interested in listening than speaking, and which led to some new thoughts and insights. He showed himself to be a leader who did not feel it necessary to put on a character, did not demand attention, did not force his ideas on others, and in fact empowered others in conversation.

That sounds a lot like Jesus!

---

[4] Jim Collins, *How the Mighty Fall* (New York: HarperCollins, 2009). Also, see http://www.jimcollins.com/books/how-the-mighty-fall.html (cited 18-Dec-2017).

Prayer:

Humble Lord Jesus,

Thank you for your example to our leading. Help us to lead like you.

Grow in us the virtue of humility. Help us to humble ourselves. Grant us also an attitude of service. Show us creative ways we might serve others.

Help us to see how we might influence others for your sake and for their sake. Help us also to be excellent followers.

Help us to glorify you, and not ourselves, in every part of our leading.

AMEN

Taking It Further:

1

Think about the second story of leadership at the beginning of the chapter. How could that person have handled the situation differently? What would you do or say in that situation?

2

Meditate on the two postures of Jesus-shaped leadership: humility and serving others. Would others describe you as humble and/or serving? How can you grow this virtue and this attitude in your life? How can you lift others up, and serve others more effectively in your role as a leader? Are you tempted to boast or bring honour to yourself?

3

Work through the passages in Matthew describing the irresistible qualities of Jesus. What do you notice on closer reading? Which aspects can you incorporate into your own life?

4

Visit Jim Collins' website and look through his articles on leadership: http://www.jimcollins.com/article_topics/articles.html#*leadership. Note which articles highlight aspects that might be congruent with Jesus-shaped leadership. Journal your learning.

Chapter 3
Beauty in the Workplace

My friend Imogen sees beauty and loves beautiful things. She uses this gift in many ways and in many places, including the workplace. I asked her how she mingles beauty and work, and she wrote the following reflection.

I gravitate towards beauty. I seem to be irresistibly attracted to beautiful things; when I find Beauty I want to surround myself with it, wrap myself in it, and wallow gloriously in whatever that particular thing is. I tend to appropriate Beauty, and I love it so much that it embeds itself into all facets of my life.

An illustration of this is the way that I experience tea. I love tea. I love everything about it. The sound the teacup makes on the saucer as you hold it, the patterns made by the steam as it curls from the spout of the teapot, the sound of the liquid pouring into the cup, the warmth, the ritual. I love tea. So I bring my favourite tea to work because I enjoy loose-leaf more than tea bags. Then I think, "I don't like the way this mug feels as I hold it", so I bring a teacup or mug from home. Then, before I know it, I have a set of teacups, a silver teapot, and five varieties of loose-leaf tea at work.

People laugh. But they linger to look, and when asked if they'd like to share the pot, there aren't many people who say no. Then, and this is the part I love most, they start to talk. It's hilarious actually. They can't seem to help themselves. The out-of-the-ordinary act of sitting at work and having tea in a beautiful way — the familiar, yet decontextualized, ritual that allows a brief change of pace prompts them to share their own passions, memories, or other points of connection with that moment.

I've never thought about consciously creating beauty at work — I just selfishly invest in curating my own micro-environment and people seem to be drawn to that. Maybe as human beings we're drawn to passion, to extra effort, to things that hint at others' hidden depths. Whatever it is, those little moments of

*beauty at worst provide moments of respite and pleasure that
are often sorely needed during the working day. But at best they
provoke something more. Sometimes it's the ability to connect
with colleagues, sometimes the provision of a sense of joy that
stains through your day, or the mental and physical space to step
back and refocus.*

*Whatever it is, you can speak about beauty at work
manifesting as clean desks that enable efficiency, or affecting
your aesthetic environment by putting up buntings or postcards.
These things are good things. But I think it goes deeper than that.
The truest beauty combines the presence of an aesthetic quality
with something more. It's up to you to figure out what that more
is. I'd start by asking the Father.*

How God Grabs Our Attention

A wise man once told me that God grabs our attention in two ways:
through suffering, and through beauty. Through the centuries,
Christians have been at the forefront of meeting the challenges and
causes of suffering in all its forms to all sorts of peoples. In the Middle
Ages and into the Renaissance, we saw Christians at the leading edge
of the arts and architecture.

However, it feels like that movement has lessened. There is much
written about God's voice being heard in suffering, but I have heard
less about the call of God through beauty.

Our appreciation of the aesthetic as people of faith has failed to
maintain its theological foundation. We may feel embarrassed at the
excesses of beauty, or concerned about its expense, or worry that a
focus on it might distract us from God.

Biblical References to Beauty

Nevertheless, when we are in nature beholding God's creation in all
its beauty, most of us know its impact on us spiritually. Certainly the
psalmists saw a direct connection between what was pleasing to the
eye and it giving glory to God.

Psalm 19:1: "The heavens declare the glory of God; the skies proclaim the work of his hands."

Psalm 29:2–3: "Ascribe to the LORD the glory due his name; worship the LORD in the splendor of his holiness. The voice of the LORD is over the waters; the God of glory thunders, the LORD thunders over the mighty waters."

Psalm 139:14: "I praise you because I am fearfully and wonderfully made; your works are wonderful, I know that full well."

Just search the internet for images of nature and you will see how prominently the beauty around us touches the minds and hearts of all people, not just believers. Indeed, Paul suggests that God made us that way: that the beauty and wonder of God's creation would be the way he reveals himself. "For since the creation of the world God's invisible qualities — his eternal power and divine nature — have been clearly seen, being understood from what has been made, so that people are without excuse" (Romans 1:20).

The writer of Ecclesiastes implies that everything is inherently beautiful, and yet we are confounded by the mystery of this: "He has made everything beautiful in its time. He has also set eternity in the human heart; yet no one can fathom what God has done from beginning to end" (Ecclesiastes 3:11).

In the New Testament, Paul tells the Ephesians that they are God's workmanship (2:10), where the Greek word used literally means God's work of art. We are each an example of God's craftsmanship.

Paul also encourages us to embrace and express beauty in his final exhortations to the Christians in Philippi: "Finally, brothers and sisters, whatever is true, whatever is noble, whatever is right, whatever is pure, whatever is lovely, whatever is admirable — if anything is excellent or praiseworthy — think about such things" (Philippians 4:8).

Beauty in the Workplace

Looking for and connecting with beauty in our workplace is one of the ways we can reveal God to others. Making our workplaces beautiful is another way we can redeem or renew our workplaces, giving people a foretaste of heaven.

When I was teaching several performing arts students an overview of the Old Testament, we had a fascinating discussion about beauty. I pointed out that God created things so that they would be pleasing to our eyes, with unnecessary diversity and wonder (Genesis 2:9).

There are several creation narratives in the Bible, but this comes through most obviously in Psalm 104. Here is just a sample from verses 24–26:

> How many are your works, LORD!
> In wisdom you made them all;
> the earth is full of your creatures.
> There is the sea, vast and spacious,
> teeming with creatures beyond number —
> living things both large and small.
> There the ships go to and fro,
> and Leviathan, which you formed to frolic there.

As I taught, I particularly focused on that moment in Israel's history when God gave Moses specific instructions for the creation of the Tent of Meeting where his presence would dwell with his people (Exodus 25ff). Even though the people were travelling through the wilderness, there were specific details given for making beautiful objects to enhance the worship of God. The making of the objects also represented a sacrifice to God.

In Exodus 39, Moses inspected all that had been done (vv. 32–43). In a scene that sounds like it is taken from Genesis 1, Moses saw what had been made, affirmed it and blessed the people. In Exodus 40, God came down to dwell in the tabernacle. He blessed the beauty with his presence.

The performing arts students discussed this concept of unnecessary beauty and how it related to their own creativity, including the connection to imagination, building a sense of community of shared appreciation, and driving a desire to excel.

The concept is also connected to finding meaning. Frederick Buechner is quoted as saying, "Beauty is to the spirit what food is to the flesh. It fills an emptiness in you which nothing else can fill."[1]

Some Ideas for Connecting with Beauty

Here are some ideas for connecting with beauty in the workplace:

- Enjoy those moments in your working when you get the opportunity to be creative. Creativity connects with imagination and allows you to reach beyond yourself.
- Think of ways you can beautify your workplace. Start with your immediate workspace, but think of ways to move beyond. Start a pot plant garden, decorate the walls, add some colour, play music, use an air freshener or fragrance diffuser, etc.
- Try to spot something that is already something beautiful in your workplace and see if you can enhance it in some way. Maybe you can accentuate a view out a window, point out some paintings, or gather chairs in a garden area.
- Attune yourself to the aesthetic. Notice interesting lines, shadows, patterns, and colours. Pay attention to every detail around you. Use all your senses: sound, smell, taste, feel, as well as sight.
- It is good to remember that beauty is one way we can give others a foretaste of what God's kingdom will be like in all its fullness and glory. We get a little glimpse of that in the description of the Holy City, the New Jerusalem, on the New Earth: "It shone with the glory of God, and its brilliance was like that of a very precious jewel, like a jasper, clear as crystal" (Revelation 21:11).

---

[1] Quoted by Luci Shaw in *The Swiftly Tilted Worlds of Madeleine L'Engle* (Wheaton: Harold Shaw, 1998), 15.

Prayer:

God of beauty and wonder,

Thank you that you didn't just make things functional, ordinary, or regular.

You made things unusual, bright, different, varied, strange, and gorgeous.

You created us as your work of art, with the ability to appreciate beauty.

Thank you that on the New Earth there will be no defects, but everything will be beautiful.

Help us to see the unnecessary beauty around us, to make our workplaces beautiful, to create beauty, and to celebrate beauty in our working.

AMEN

Taking It Further:

1

Look for images of beauty on the Internet that you can collect and reflect on. They might be images of nature, people, paintings, or designs. Alternatively, collect music that you consider beautiful into a playlist. Note down your responses to the images or sounds. Allow your appreciation to move into appreciation of the Creator.

2

Make a list of everything that is chaotic, ugly, or defective about your workplace or working. Make a list of everything that is beautiful.

3

Psalm 90:17 says: "May the favor *(beauty)* of the Lord our God rest on us; establish the work of our hands for us — yes, establish the work of our hands." In *The Message,* Eugene Peterson translates those verses as: "And let the loveliness of our Lord, our God, rest on us, confirming the work that we do. Oh, yes. Affirm the work that we do!" What would it mean to apply these verses in your workplace?

4

Build on Activity 2 and go through the list of suggestions on connecting with beauty. List the ways you can bring order or make things more beautiful. How can you make your workplace flourish? What are the short-term actions? What might take more time or planning?

Chapter 4
Ethical
Decision-Making

Three Ethical Challenges at Work

Christie worked in sales for a large toy-making company. She enjoyed her job which involved plenty of travel and playing with the products to get to know them. We talked a few times about applying her faith to her job, and she was really challenged. She could not work out how to do her job without exaggerating the benefits of the product, and misleading outlets about the deals she had with their competitors. She seemed very comfortable with being a Christian and basically lying.

Sheryl and her husband worked in the construction business and had a great team working for them. Their problem was also with clients. In one case there was a client who was not paying their bills, so Sheryl instructed her employees to withdraw from the site and held the client to ransom until they were willing to pay the bills. When asked about how she felt that act reflected on her organisation as a Christian business, she said, "Well, there are times when you are Christian and there are times when you just have to play by the rules of business."

Jonathan worked with a Christian organisation in Bangalore, India, but his ethical dilemma was a very private matter. His father had died of natural causes, and when Jonathan went to request the body from the morgue to bury his father, the morgue manager refused to release the body unless a large bribe was paid. The memorial service had been planned, the grave was dug, and people were waiting. Jonathan reluctantly paid the bribe, but then felt guilty about participating in unethical business practices.

Different Approaches to Ethical Decision-Making

There are different ways to making decisions about what is right and wrong. Michael Cafferky in his book, *Business Ethics in Biblical Perspective*, summarises some of the main approaches:

- Egoism: what is best for me
- Relativism: society determines what is right and wrong
- Common sense: intuition and social reasoning
- Utilitarianism: the greatest good for the greatest number

- Universalism: human reasoning
- Agency: what the government says
- Justice and rights: what is fair to others
- Virtues and character: the common good[1]

Christian Approaches

There have been various attempts to identify models for Christians to help them know how to respond to difficult decisions. There is a common ethical decision-making model based on the *Commands* of the Bible and the *Consequences* of the decision, and rooted in the *Character* of the decision-maker. It is a good guide and can lead to helpful questions and perspectives on an issue. Gordon Preece has summarised this as rules, results, and roles.[2]

Australian author Andrew Cameron in *Joined-Up Life*, introduces a model based on the *Character* of God, the nature of *Creation*, the *Commands* of the Bible, the perspective of the *New Creation*, and all under the lordship of *Christ*.[3]

The issue of character is very helpful when considering whether or not our decisions reflect Christ. While there are various lists of virtues, the fruit of the Spirit are a helpful guide (Galatians 5:22-23). Are our actions loving, peaceful, coming from a joyful heart, patient, kind, good, faithful, gentle, and self-controlled?

Evaluating Ethical Issues

When looking particularly at possible ethical issues at work, we may find them to vary considerably.

Michael Cafferky suggests the following categorisation for us to work out how much is at stake:

---

[1] Michael Cafferky, *Business Ethics in Biblical Perspective* (Downers Grove: InterVarsity Press, 2015).
[2] Gordon Preece, "Mind the Moral Gap: A Relational Ethical Framework", https://www.christiansuper.com.au/files/Philosophical%20Ethical%20Framework%20-%20Gordon%20Preece.pdf (cited 18-Dec-2017).
[3] Andrew Cameron, *Joined-Up Life* (UK: InterVarsity Press, 2011).

- *Simple and easy*: stealing from the organisation
- *Complicated and difficult*: using work's Wi-Fi for Facebook
- *More complicated and difficult*: working in marketing and getting fired for refusing to fly out of a fear of flying
- *Even more complicated and difficult*: the government proposing to raise its Goods and Services Tax with a significant impact on your small business
- *Most complicated and difficult*: responding to climate change issues[4]

The most common approach to determining whether a decision is ethical at work is consideration of the consequences:

- Identify the action that can be taken
- Identify relevant alternatives to the action
- Evaluate foreseeable benefits and harms
- Choose the alternative that gives the best outcomes

There are many problems with this approach. What if there are unforeseeable consequences? What if the benefits and harms cannot be quantified? What if you are biased toward a certain approach and tempted to exaggerate the outcomes?

The reality is that we often make poor decisions because we cannot be objective, because we are rushed, because we go by the letter of the law rather than the spirit of the law, and because we excuse a decision on the basis of "it's just part of the job".

A Biblical Framework

Michael Cafferky has come up with a much more biblically-based Values Framework for considering the decisions we might make. It can be summarised as a series of questions, which I have adapted here:

---

[4] Michael Cafferky, *Business Ethics in Biblical Perspective* (Downer Groves: InterVarsity Press, 2015), 73.

- Is it creative and sustaining? (Creation)
- Is it the right thing to do? (Holiness)
- Does it enhance relationship? (Relationship)
- Will it lead to flourishing? (Shalom)
- Is it a just thing to do? (Justice)
- Does it have integrity? (Truth)
- Is it a wise thing to do? (Wisdom)
- Does it show compassion? (Love)
- Does it set someone free? (Redemption)[5]

If Christie from the toy-making company applied this framework, she might come up with an entirely different set of actions. Her decision to do or say anything to get a sale may have short-term benefits but long-term consequences.

It is probably not sustainable to continue lying and pretending. It is certainly not a holy thing to do, because we know the Bible explicitly forbids lying. It does not enhance her relationship with her customers, because it is a relationship based on lies rather than trust. It will not lead to flourishing because it is a manipulative action. It is not a just thing to do, because the determined price is based on false premises and differs between customers. It is not based on truth. It is not wise, because once found out, it will impact on Christie's reputation and the reputation of her organisation. It does not demonstrate love, since her desire is to trick and manipulate the customer for personal gain. Finally, her behaviour actually binds her, because she is fearful of being found out, and it restricts the freedom of the customer also.

Steps to an Ethical Decision

When faced with a difficult ethical decision, take the following steps to help you make the best decision possible:

---

[5] Michael Cafferky, *Business Ethics in Biblical Perspective* (Downers Grove: InterVarsity Press, 2015). See Chapter 4, "Biblical Themes for Business Ethics".

- **Stop and think:** don't be tempted to rush a difficult ethical decision; it is better to take time and make a solid decision
- **Determine the facts:** make sure you have all information needed
- **Think through the Values Framework:** ask the questions that are listed above
- **Develop options:** while being conscious that you must also represent the needs of your organisation
- **Consider consequences:** try to be creative about possible even if improbable consequences
- **Ask questions:** make sure you involve the key people making or being impacted by the decision
- **Monitor and modify:** don't feel that you cannot change tack; too many poor decisions are made worse by people too proud to modify the decision after the event

A wise man once told me that the final question he asked himself when making a difficult decision is: "How will I feel if that decision is portrayed as the lead story on a digital news source tomorrow morning?"

Prayer:

Dear Lord,

You know the difficulty and complexity of the issues we face, and the way we struggle to make good decisions.

Sometimes we do not have much power to influence decisions.

Sometimes we feel compelled to make what we know are poor decisions because we might lose face, we are competing with others, or we are fearful of retribution.

Please grant us the courage to make not just the best decision, but the right decision, the good decision, and the wise decision.

Help us to grow as ethical decision-makers, considering the consequences on people and the rest of your creation.

AMEN

Taking It Further:

1

Look at the first list of bullet points. Which of the different approaches to decision-making are you tempted to make? Which is the approach you see most often used in your workplace? Or used as a justification?

2

Think of a difficult ethical decision you have made lately. Go through the Values Framework questions, and determine whether the decision you made was the best decision you could have made. What might you do differently? What other options have opened up?

3

Search through the Bible to find verses that match the different values listed in the framework.

4

Think of a difficult ethical decision you have to make, or are likely to make soon. Go through the process listed at the end of the chapter. What further information will you need to gather? How has the Values Framework changed your thinking? What are the challenges and benefits of this new approach to ethical decision-making?

Chapter 5
Dealing with Stress

Recently, I taught a Masters class of students who had been asked to survey church congregations on the most difficult issues they faced as Christians in the workplace.

In reverse order, number 3 was *conflict* at work, with workplace Christians conscious that they should be peacemakers, yet facing the reality that it is difficult for people to always get along in the pressure of work.

Number 2 was *ethical challenges*, with workplace Christians reporting difficulties in navigating the murky ethical issues of working, while upholding biblical standards.

However, the most outstanding issue for these workplace Christians, by far, was *handling work stress*. They reported feeling stretched and overwhelmed by the pressures of work, and finding it difficult to find a balance.

Stress at Work

Christians in the workplace are not the only ones feeling the stress of working. A 2015 stress and wellbeing survey by the Australian Psychological Society found a trending increase in workplace stress and anxiety, with 45% of Australians complaining of work-related stress. A report from 2008 claimed it was costing Australia almost $15 billion a year due to absenteeism, or presenteeism — that is, people impacted by stress but turning up to work only to do sub-par work. Direct costs from stress claims compensation is a further $10 billion. There are also hidden costs in re-skilling or restaffing due to high turnovers.[1]

It is important to realise that not all stress is bad. All of us need some level of stress to get us motivated and productive. This is called eustress. At some point — and this will differ individually — the amount of stress becomes negative on our effectiveness, and we become distressed.

---

[1] "Stress and wellbeing in Australia survey 2015", Australian Psychological Society. https://www.headsup.org.au/docs/default-source/default-document-library/stress-and-wellbeing-in-australia-report.pdf?sfvrsn=7f08274d_4 (accessed 21-Mar-2018).

What Causes Stress at Work (Stressors)

- ❯ Work factors, such as long working hours or unreasonable performance expectations.
- ❯ The physical environment of the workplace, especially if it is crowded, noisy, unsafe, or holds risk of repetitive injuries.
- ❯ Work organisational practices, such as a lack of control over one's work, poor communication, or a lack of clarity about roles and responsibilities.
- ❯ Changes at work, resulting in insecurity, high turnover, or stifled opportunity for promotion.
- ❯ Issues with workplace relationships, including bullying, office politics, conflict, or competition.

The impact of stress can move through nervousness and a feeling of being overwhelmed, to tension and strain (expressed internally and/or in work and family relationships), to anxiety (including panic attacks) and depression, to perhaps even suicidal impulse. Health symptoms related to stress include insomnia, headaches, gastrointestinal discomfort, and even heart problems.

A Snapshot of Suffering from Work Stress

Joanne was feeling lots of stress at work induced by changes in leadership, lack of consultation about her workload, and the threat of job cutbacks. In addition, there was the breakdown of a few key workplace relationships.

Joanne was suffering from sleep deprivation, waking up only to be distracted by work worries. She also had increasing stomach irritation and occasionally felt her heart racing.

She was also often grumpy toward others at home, and sometimes used wine as self-medication to cope with the feeling of being overwhelmed.

She suffered from these symptoms for three months before realising she needed to ask for help. She went to a doctor, who recommended a psychologist, who then painfully rebuilt Joanne's sense of esteem and wellbeing. Having a supportive family also greatly helped. It took her 12 months before she felt able to deal with the stress of her workplace.

At first, Joanne was angry with God for allowing her to get into that situation in the first place, but over time she found God's presence to be a great source of solace and comfort. Nevertheless, she often felt depleted at church, and incapable of participating in church activities. It was something Joanne found difficult to discuss with her church friends, feeling embarrassed at her inability to cope at work.

Joanne's story is quite typical, but also very sad. She hesitated telling others about her struggles out of fear of the stigma of stress as a mental illness. She waited too long to get assistance, and by then the situation was spiralling downward both at work and at home. The stress impacted on her spiritual relationships and her capacity to serve in the church community.

Dealing with Work Stress

Here are some ideas for dealing with stress in the workplace. First are the normal stress-management tips:

- Eat well, get enough sleep, and make sure you exercise for at least 30 minutes a day, at least five times a week.
- Inform your supervisor of your symptoms, and seek to gain more control over your working environment, especially regarding performance expectations.
- Make sure you practise self-control rather than react impulsively to colleagues and family members. See those connections as supporters rather than enemies. This will help to maximise your assistance and minimise conflict at work and home.

- Find someone who will actively listen to your struggles and validate your feelings, as well as help you commit to measures to better manage, or reduce the stressors.
- Focus on relaxing hobbies or activities.
- Avoid relying on alcohol, gambling, or drugs. These are commonly used to numb the pain of stress but they are not effective at increasing your ability to deal with stress, and may lead to addictions and even worse health, social, and psychological problems.

A Christian Approach to Managing Stress
Secondly, here are several spiritual stress management tips:

- Pray through the stress, even when you are not conscious of God hearing your prayers. If possible, have others who will commit to pray *for*, or preferably *with* you.
- Remember that your identity, esteem, and security need to be found *in Christ* rather than in your work. You are God's child, made in his image with eternal hope. What happens at work cannot impact or alter these truths.
- Keep a Sabbath, a weekly time of rest and focus on God that acts as a contrast to the stress of work. Let it be a time of preparation for the week ahead, as well as of genuine gratitude to God for his mercies, provision, and sustenance.
- There is much in Scripture encouraging us to cast our anxieties on God because he cares for us (1 Peter 5:7) and will take our burdens upon himself. Eugene Peterson beautifully paraphrases Matthew 11:28-30 in *The Message*: "Are you tired? Worn out? Burned out on religion? Come to me. Get away with me and you'll recover your life. I'll show you how to take a real rest. Walk with me and work with me —watch how I do it. Learn the unforced rhythms of grace. I won't lay anything heavy or ill-fitting on you. Keep company with me and you'll learn to live freely and lightly."
- Biblical stories are also a source of encouragement. Consider David's confidence in God in the midst of his stress as he flees from

Saul, expressed in Psalms 7, 27, 31, and 34. We also see a godly response in Jesus as he wrestled with his impending arrest, trial, death, and separation from God in the Garden of Gethsemane (Matthew 26:36–46). As he prayed, he told God his frustrations and fears, yet submitted to God's will.

In his excellent book, *Under Pressure*, Andrew Laird describes the different Christian postures that help us to cope with the stress and pressures of work:

- We don't need to have it all because we have an all-powerful, eternal God who promises us that the best is yet to come.
- Jesus invites us to live in a less-pressured way.
- We can lean in with love when dealing with the pressure of difficult workplace relationships.
- We do not have to conform to the workplace.
- We can relinquish our desire to be on top of everything.
- We are part of the body of Christ, and can draw on the support and wisdom of our brothers and sisters in church.[2]

---

[2] Andrew Laird, *Under Pressure* (Australia: City Bible Forum, 2017), 105–106.

Prayer:

God of rest and comfort,

It is such a relief that you do not measure us by what we achieve, or how short our to do list is, or the number of perfect scores on our performance reviews.

You are much more concerned about our hearts and whether we are devoted to you.

You love it when we flourish.

You delight when our purposes align with your purposes for the world.

Please help us to recognise when we are pushing ourselves for the idols of success, excellence, status, or security.

Help us to see when we are at the edge of burnout.

Help us to prioritise resting in you, and taking good care of the bodies you have given us.

Help us to model sensible working with others.

AMEN

Taking It Further:

1

Take an online stress test to measure your own vulnerability. There are many, but this is a quick one: http://www.stress.org.uk/individual-stress-test/. Discuss the results with a friend or family member.

2

Make a list of all the things that make you uncomfortable or feel pressured at work (work through the stressors in this chapter). Make a list of the ways you would prefer things to be. Is there anything you can change? What behaviours could you change? Can you discuss the list with your supervisor or colleagues?

3

Work through the Psalms and note down key encouraging verses you can refer to when you feel overwhelmed or under pressure. Put them on cards and cycle through them in your wallet. Or laminate a few and put them up in your office space.

4

Read Joanne's story again. How would you care for her if you were her colleague? Do you notice anyone at your workplace stressed out like Joanne? Who is vulnerable? What could you do to help?

Chapter 6
Work-Life Balance

Why can't we have it all?

There is so much that we want out of life:

- A comfortable life with adequate material possessions, at the minimum a nice house, functional car, good education for us and our kids, sufficient holidays, up-to-date technology.
- A fulfilling romantic relationship, preferably leading to offspring.
- Positive relationships with our family and supportive friends.
- A challenging and interesting career, including professional development, some travel, and access to promotions.
- Opportunity to pursue leisure activities, sports, and/or hobbies.
- Good health, with physical and mental ability to maximise opportunities to enjoy life.
- Opportunity to belong to a vibrant Christian community with excellent Bible teaching and heart-stirring worship.

Striving for all these gets exhausting, especially since many of them are outside our control such as meeting the right partner, having children, and maintaining good health. Also, many of them do not have limits. For example, defining a comfortable life depends on where we live and whom we compare ourselves to; and our concept of necessities for comfort will tend to expand as we get older.

A Biblical View on Our Desires

What is more, not many of these desires stand up to biblical scrutiny. We are never promised a comfortable life, fulfilling relationships, meaningful work or play, perfect health, or a church that meets our needs. By contrast, we are invited to join Christ in his suffering (1 Peter 4:12–13), to work with what we have (1 Corinthians 4:12), to serve others rather than seek to be served (Mark 10:45), and to be content whatever the circumstances (Philippians 4:11–12).

The temptation to have it all can easily lead to drivenness, where we lose sight of God and others in our desire to either accumulate wealth or make a name for ourselves.

How Driven Are You at Work?

Here are good questions to check how much your work controls you.

- How do you value your work: by how much you are paid, or by how your work aligns with what God values?
- Do you depend on work or on God? Do you work to increase your sense of self-worth?
- How demanding is your work? Does it take precedence over faith and/or family?
- How much do you allow work to intrude into your life? Do you check emails or answer calls when at home, on weekends, or on holidays?
- How much do you use work to avoid your other responsibilities or issues? Is it a means of avoiding a deeper faith, or family relationships? Does your working hard mask a failure to deal with other issues or addictions?

The Empty Promise of Work Idolatry

I had a good friend whose father worked really hard for a chemical engineering factory. He spent long days at work, and my friend and her brother hardly saw him when they were growing up. His wife, their mother, sadly was diagnosed with cancer while they were children. At last, he took his eyes off work. But it was too late. She died, and he was already estranged from the children.

One day, after her dad had retired, he came to her ashen-faced. He had been sitting on the train going past his old workplace — and it was gone. The factory was completely knocked down and the metal and bricks taken offsite. All that was left was a hole in the ground. He came to his daughter to apologise for all the time he spent at work when he should have been spending time with her.

Achieving More Balance
A right attitude
The first step to achieving work–life balance is to ensure that we have a

right attitude toward work, and life, as gifts from God to be used in his service as acts of worship. It is that offering of our work which lasts, not the physical place of our working.

A biblical view of rest and play[1]

One of the fundamental concepts of rest is that God has set an example for us in resting. In Genesis 2:2–3, we see God resting from the work he had done. This was enshrined in the Ten Commandments, as a way of honouring God (Exodus 20:8–11). As Jesus pointed out, this concept of the Sabbath was also made for our sake (Mark 2:27).

Another way of looking at rest is in the chronology of creation: human beings were made on the 6th day, rested with God on the 7th, then worked from the 8th. Rest is something we do to work effectively.

God has also created us with playful hearts. I love the way Jesus had a balance between teaching, praying, and playing. He socialised, went to weddings, invited people to dinner, and seemed to enjoy just hanging out with people. He went boating, walking, and climbing.

There are two dangers in our attitude to play. One is that we enjoy play too much, "amusing ourselves to death" as Neil Postman warned; we cry out to be entertained, as Nirvana sang. The second danger is that we work at our leisure such that we rob it of its playful and recreational nature. I see people slaving at fitness, ticking off a bucket list of activities, and seeking adrenalin-fuelled pursuits. We need to do leisure activities that are fun, develop our gifts, increase our capacity, and enhance our relationships.

Reordering Our Priorities for Balance[2]

However, to achieve balance, we need to do more than merely share out work, rest, and play. We need to know what is important to God. That means we need a biblical view of home and community, to sustain

---

[1] This material on play is influenced by the chapter "Play" in the *Complete Book of Everyday Christianity*, edited by Robert Banks and R. Paul Stevens (Singapore: Graceworks, 2011).

[2] This helpful material was prepared by Dr Ken Barnes, as part of an unpublished Bible studies series on work–life balance.

us socially and be a place of sanctuary, respect, and grace; of our own relationship with God, as we seek to be in the centre of his will and plan for us; and of our physical health, ensuring we get sufficient exercise and sleep, and eat well.

We also need to seek God's guidance in managing our priorities. God gives us the responsibility of being good stewards of our time, our talent, and our treasure, but provides much guidance in his Word.

Stewarding our time
In stewarding our time, we should read the Bible (2 Timothy 3:16–17), pray (Mark 1:35), seek to build the kingdom (Matthew 28:18–20), work well (1 Corinthians 4:12; 2 Thessalonians 3:6–8), and rest (Exodus 20:8–11).

Stewarding our talents
In stewarding our talents, we should make sure we worship God (Colossians 3:17, 23), serve others (1 Peter 4:10; like Jesus: Mark 10:45), teach (Colossians 1:28), care (Acts 4:32–35), be creative (Exodus 31:1–5), and use our gifts (1 Corinthians 12:4–7).

Stewarding our treasure
In stewarding our treasure, we need to ensure we tithe (Leviticus 27:30; 2 Corinthians 8:1–13), provide for our family (1 Timothy 5:8), provide for others in need (Ephesians 4:28), and protect creation (Genesis 1:26).

Prayer:

To the God of rest,

We are so busy with our working and playing, with all that needs to be done.

Yet you never seem to be rushing in your creating, but you are patient.

Jesus also seemed to be calm and careful.

Forgive us for our wilfulness, our desire to control all things, and our lack of satisfaction.

Help us to reorder ourselves around you and your timing.

Help us to know your priorities.

Grant us such balanced lives that there is time for you, and time for others, and time for renewing our heart, mind, body, and spirit.

AMEN

Taking It Further:

1

Look at the first list of bullet points, at the things we want for our lives. How many of those things are the desires of your heart? Which ones would be hard to release? Take time to hand them over to God. Ask God to provide you with what you need. Be encouraged by these words from 1 Timothy 6:17: "Command those who are rich in this present world not to be arrogant nor to put their hope in wealth, which is so uncertain, but to put their hope in God, who richly provides us with everything for our enjoyment."

2

Go through the set of questions to test your own attitude to your working. Which questions did you find difficult to answer? In what ways were you encouraged? In what ways were you challenged? What should you change as a result of your responses?

3

Work through the stewardship Bible verses listed in the chapter. Make a list of your priorities versus God's priorities in the areas of stewarding time, talent, and treasure. What could change? What can you continue to build on?

4

Write a letter to someone who knows you well (partner, child, parent, pastor, friend, or even God) and write down the ways that you are going to reorient your life to achieve greater balance. Ask them to follow up with you in six months to test whether you have kept to these commitments.

Chapter 7

Handling Bullying and Conflict

(Much of the material in this chapter initially appeared on the Fixing Her Eyes *website[1])*

Jackie was excited about landing her dream job teaching at a Christian school. But reasonably quickly the situation began to deteriorate. No one explained to her how things worked, so she was constantly having to ask questions which were responded to curtly.

She had a particular clash with one staff member and when she asked their common manager to intervene, he asked her instead to explain **her** actions. Jackie pulled out her position description to demonstrate she actually had authority over the disputed situation. The manager admitted she was right, but no one apologised and the tension continued. After several months, she was on the receiving end of an angry outburst from a fellow teacher. From that incident, she discovered that there was resentment by that teacher in particular, but also more generally by the staff, about the manner of her appointment. The correct procedures had not been followed.

Her manager had agreed that her workload was too much, but when giving her the much requested administration support, he also gave her a new project. When she explained her inability to complete the extra project because of a focus on other tasks and marketing, he told her to stop marketing. Three months later, she was told that lack of income generated from marketing meant her role was being cut back.

There were a hundred other little cuts: her name left off lists of staff; no room allocated at a staff retreat; being told she was not qualified to apply for a higher duties job she was already doing for a year, and that job then given to a less qualified and less experienced man; asked to address a group, and then not being invited to present; ignored in a meeting when she said something, only to have someone else say the same thing and be affirmed; being told her contract would not be renewed, but that she was not allowed to inform anyone beyond immediate family.

---

[1] *Fixing Her Eyes*, http://www.fixinghereyes.org/read-all/author/Kara-Martin.

While each of these situations might not be considered particularly harmful individually, the combined force can be seen to be part of a systematic issue of bullying, particularly by Jackie's manager.

Defining Workplace Bullying

Bullying is repeated, unreasonable behaviour directed toward a worker, or group of workers, that creates a risk to health and safety. It includes behaviours such as:

- Abusive, insulting, or offensive language or comments.
- Malicious sarcasm.
- Unjustified criticism or complaints.
- Spreading misinformation or malicious rumours.
- Deliberately excluding someone from workplace activities.
- Withholding information that is vital for effective work performance.
- Setting unreasonable timelines or constantly changing deadlines.
- Denying access to information, supervision, consultation, or resources to the detriment of the worker.
- Unreasonable treatment in relation to accessing entitlements such as leave and training.
- Interfering with someone's personal property or work equipment.[2]

Positive Workplace Culture

Bullying can also be contrasted with a positive workplace culture, which will:

- Ensure the dignity of all employees at work.
- Ensure fair and just dealings.
- Build happy and constructive working relationships.

---

[2] This definition is from a document: "Workplace bullying: Violence, Harassment, and Bullying Fact sheet", *Australian Human Rights Commission*. https://www.humanrights.gov.au/workplace-bullying-violence-harassment-and-bullying-fact-sheet (cited 7-Feb-2018). It is a standard for Australian workplaces.

- Ensure respect is shown and differences valued.
- Encourage constructive discussion of differences of views and approaches.
- Ensure open and constructive communications.
- Prevent actions of bullying, exclusion, unfair treatment, and other negative or demeaning behaviours.
- Deal firmly and fairly with negative behaviours, including bullying and harassment.[3]

Christians may further face the challenge of being victimised for their faith, a situation that has been reported several times in groups I have spoken to.

How Bullying Can Affect Your Work

If you are being bullied at work you might:

- Be less active or successful.
- Be less confident in your work.
- Feel scared, stressed, anxious, or depressed.
- Have your life outside of work affected, e.g. study, relationships.
- Want to stay away from work.
- Feel like you can't trust your employer or the people whom you work with.
- Lack confidence and happiness about yourself and your work.
- Have physical signs of stress like headaches, backaches, sleep problems.[4]

Bullying is a significant problem in the wider workforce. The Australian Workplace Barometer reported that, "There is a serious

---

[3] For more ideas about anti-bullying policies, see: "Preventing bullying at work", *Worksafe Victoria*, October 2010. https://www.worksafe.vic.gov.au/__data/assets/pdf_file/0013/11191/MIA_bullying_Final.pdf (cited 18-Dec-2017).

[4] See: Workplace bullying: Violence, Harassment, and Bullying Fact sheet", *Australian Human Rights Commission*. https://www.humanrights.gov.au/workplace-bullying-violence-harassment-and-bullying-fact-sheet (cited 18-Dec-2017).

concern regarding levels of bullying and harassment. Results from the AWB show that levels of bullying are at 6.8%, which are substantially higher than international rates." Those 6.8% experienced bullying in the previous six months, and more than half said that bullying had been continuing for longer than six months.[5]

Such statistics do not tell the whole picture, since generally bullying and mental health issues are under-reported. In the United States 45% of workers say they have experienced workplace abuse.[6]

Dealing with Workplace Bullying

Dr Michelle Callahan in the *Huffington Post* gives an excellent list of tips for dealing with bullying:

1. **Don't get emotional.** Bullies take pleasure in emotionally manipulating people. Stay calm and rational to diffuse the situation.
2. **Don't blame yourself.** Acknowledge that this is not about you; it's about the bully.
3. **Do your best work.** The bully's behaviour will seem more justified if you aren't doing your best work, or if you do things like come to work late, take long lunches, turn in work late, etc.
4. **Build a support network.** Instead of hiding or retreating into your office, work on building your relationships with your co-workers so that you have support.
5. **Document everything.** Keep a journal (on your personal computer or in writing, but never leave it in the office) of what happened when (and who witnessed it). Keep emails and notes.

---

[5] Maureen Dollard et al., "The Australian Workplace Barometer: Report on psychosocial safety climate and worker health in Australia" (Magill: Safe Work Australia, 2012), 59.
[6] Michelle Callahan, "10 Tips for Dealing with Bullies at Work", *The Huffington Post*, 17 November 2011. http://www.huffingtonpost.com/dr-michelle-callahan/work-bullies_b_833977.html (cited 18-Dec-2017).

6. **Seek help.** If you think you're being bullied, it's time to start talking to others who can help you manage this situation. Try a mentor, advocate, seasoned/experienced friend, even a legal advocate who specialises in bullying and inappropriate or discriminatory behaviour in the workplace.

7. **Get counselling.** It will help you deal with the stress, especially if the bullying is already affecting your physical and mental health. You have to take care of yourself.

8. **Stay healthy.** Maintain a balanced lifestyle outside of work to help you cope with the madness at work. Work out, get a good night's sleep, and eat a healthy diet.

9. **Educate yourself.** Learn everything you can about bullying, your company's policies on inappropriate behaviour and occupational law regarding this kind of experience.

10. **Don't expect to change the bully.** Real behaviour change is difficult and it takes time. You have no control over a bully's willingness to accept that they have a problem and to work on it. In the worst-case scenario you may need to leave your job.[7]

A Christian Perspective

For Christians, there are some tensions:

> Jesus told us to turn the other cheek, but tough love may involve standing up to the bully.

> There is a desire for revenge that is palpable, but it must be offset by a desire for righteousness.

> We are told to love our enemies, but how is that balanced by our godly fight for justice?

---

[7] Michelle Callahan, "10 Tips for Dealing with Bullies at Work", *The Huffington Post*, 17 November 2011. http://www.huffingtonpost.com/dr-michelle-callahan/work-bullies_b_833977.html (cited 18-Dec-2017).

The Bible reveals to us some of the causes of bullying behaviour:

- In the case of Joseph, it was **jealousy** from his brothers, which was inflamed by his prideful behaviour (Genesis 37).
- Goliath was convinced that his **power** could be used to bully anyone he wanted to, and which ironically made him vulnerable to young David and his slingshot (1 Samuel 17).
- The victim in Jesus' parable of the Good Samaritan was picked on by thieves and robbers, and ignored by the religious establishment, because he was **vulnerable** as a single man travelling a dangerous road (Luke 10:25–37).
- Jesus was bullied perhaps more than anyone else in the Bible. We have graphic descriptions of his abuse and punishment including mocking, swearing, lashings, beatings, and then the horrific humiliation of the cross. It appears that those who treated him so poorly were mostly **afraid** of him, his wisdom, his miracles, his authority, his disciples, his popularity, and his claims to be the Christ (Matthew 27:11–56).

Responding to Workplace Bullying as a Christian

So how do we respond to bullying and conflict from a Christian perspective? David Augsburger offers the following excellent guidelines:

- Conflict allows us to grow more like Christ (2 Corinthians 12:7–10).
- Peacemaking starts with our personal attitude, which in turn comes from a focus on God, not on the conflict (1 Peter 3:13–15).
- It is possible to reconcile unilaterally, but only if the past is forgiven completely (Philippians 4:2–9).
- Resolving conflict may require different methods at different times and places (1 Samuel 25:26–35; Esther 7:1–6; Proverbs 6:1–5; Acts 16:22–24; 22:22–23, 29).
- Differences of opinion are inevitable and usually acceptable (1 Corinthians 12).

- Reconciliation does not necessarily require giving up or giving in; loving confrontation may be preferable (Galatians 6:1–5).
- God reconciled all to himself, but we must pass this gift on to others to fully realise its benefits (Ephesians 4:29–32).
- Resolving conflict God's way may require us to accept consequences and alter our behaviour (Ephesians 4:22–32).
- Justice is God's, not ours (Luke 6:27–39).

Biblical peacemaking involves an active commitment to restore damaged relationships and have agreements that are just and satisfactory to everyone involved (1 John 3:18). A spirit of forgiveness, open communication, and cooperative negotiation may clear away the hardness of hearts left by conflict, and make possible reconciliation and genuine personal peace. True biblical vulnerability, honesty, and forgiveness can restore a person's sense of value, both to God and to others, and lead to complete restoration of relationships (Galatians 6:1–3; Ephesians 4:1–3, 24).[8]

---

[8] In "Workplace Conflict" in *The Complete Book of Everyday Christianity*. Edited by Robert Banks and R. Paul Stevens (Singapore: Graceworks, 2011), 212–213.

Prayer:

To the one who loves peace and justice,

Forgive us when our lack of imagination or creativity stops us from seeing the way of peace.

Help us to be firm when we should stand.

Help us to be flexible when it is not our place to claim.

Help us to love you, and to love others, with our thoughts, words, and actions.

Thank you that suffering and conflict can bear fruit in us.

Help us to be peacemakers, and to stand up for justice.

Help us to remember Jesus when we have a desire for revenge.

AMEN

Taking It Further:

1

Have you ever experienced bullying or seen it happen to someone close to you? What was the nature of the bullying? What were the consequences? Do you feel Dr Callahan's 10 points would have made a difference?

2

Look through the biblical examples of those who faced bullying. Choose one to examine in more detail. What parts of the story do you identify with? How could you use this story in helping to counsel others?

3

Work through the Scripture readings in David Augsburger's guidelines on responding to conflict and being a peacemaker. What deeper insights do you glean for a biblical response to conflict?

4

Read Jackie's story again. Imagine that she has come to you for advice in the midst of her experience of bullying. Write out the conversation you would have with her.

Chapter 8
Toxic Workplaces

I had been invited to preach at an inner-city church on the good of work. Afterwards the minister took me aside and asked if he could introduce me to his daughter who worked for a prestigious management consulting company. He was concerned that she was struggling in her job, and it was impacting her faith.

I met Louise and she was delightful, but there was a tightness about her face which I recognised. She was someone who was holding her outer self together. I asked her about her work. She explained that she enjoyed the work itself, but the workplace was becoming increasingly difficult. She felt there was a complete mismatch with her values and the values of the organisation.

She was being encouraged to cut corners to save money, to overinflate good results and cover up or minimise bad results, and to convince clients to take on additional work that they didn't really need. Several times, she protested these directives but had been over-ruled, and now her team did not trust her.

She felt isolated, and did not feel valued for the good work she was doing. There was a growing sense that she was being squeezed out, made to feel so uncomfortable that she would have to leave.

By chance she had found someone else in the organisation also concerned about the company's culture. While it had been a relief to find someone else who felt the same, now she felt even more conflicted.

Would God want her to stay and fight? To make a difference for the clients who hired her? Was there a way of changing the corporate culture? If she left, would that be removing Christian influence from the organisation? What about this other worker — should she stay to support him?

We talked for a while, and I shared my ultimatum in such situations. Stay, pray, and persevere as long as you can, especially if you have good support, but if you feel the battle is impacting on your soul — the deep connection with God that keeps you grounded — then leave.

It was at that point that she told me another point of pressure in terms of her work: she didn't want to disappoint her father who had been so excited about her getting the role. Leaving would impact her career and the success he had invested in. I was able to reassure her of his concern for her, and encouraged her to speak openly with him.

Toxic versus Flourishing

Workplaces can become toxic — literally poisonous to people, not just in their ability to do work, but also in their health and wellbeing. Sometimes the toxicity can extend to clients, customers, suppliers... all those impacted by the organisation.

A toxic workplace is not just a place routinely impacted by sin. It is a place that negatively impacts on people to such an extent that it hardly seems sustainable. It goes against God's vision for business, which is the flourishing of the workers and of innovation in products and services that add to creation.

Louise was not the only one affected, but often silence is mistaken for complicity. She was also not simply uncomfortable because of her Christian faith; the organisation was disingenuous in its dealings with clients as well as employees.

The occurrence of toxic workplaces is quite widespread. I know a teacher who is feeling desperate in her school, as a new principal has caused major divisions among staff and parents. Her job is crumbling around her, and she is finding her self-confidence being undermined.

In her case, as in Louise's, there is a sense of being trapped. Louise didn't want to let her parents down. The teacher faces demotion if she leaves, and the possibility of a new posting a long way from home.

How to Know If Your Workplace Is Toxic

It may be easy to jump to the conclusion that a workplace is toxic. Sometimes the reality is that we are the wrong fit for the job. We cannot use the description toxic when we are the only one impacted, or if the workplace is simply not the way we would like it to be. Chapman, White, and Myra in their book, *Rising Above a Toxic Workplace,* describe ten signs of a toxic workplace:

1. Hidden agendas characterise communication and decision-making.
2. Departments not working together, with no shared goals.
3. Leaders say one thing but do another.
4. There is pressure to make things look good.
5. The focus is on tasks not people.
6. Workers are manipulated through embarrassment or anger.
7. People are apathetic, cynical, or lack hope.
8. Rules and procedures are mostly ignored.
9. There is no accountability for decisions.
10. People feel 'used' by the organisation, and are discarded when no longer useful.[1]

A Biblical Perspective on Toxic Cultures

There are toxic cultures described in the Bible. For example, during the time of the judges, "everyone did as they saw fit" (Judges 21:25), which included worshipping other gods, temple prostitution, child sacrifice, rape, abuse, civil war, murder, among other things.

There also must have been a toxic culture in the Corinthian church, for Paul wrote to try to correct some of the issues reported to him: infighting and factionalism (1 Corinthians 1:12); sexual immorality including incest (1 Corinthians 5:1) and prostitution (1 Corinthians 6:16–18); trying to settle disputes outside the church (1 Corinthians 6:5–7); too much focus on their bodies rather than God (implied by 1 Corinthians 6:19–20 and 10:31); chaotic church practices (1 Corinthians 11); and doubt of Paul's legitimacy and authority (2 Corinthians 10–13).

Paul's solution was to pray, name what was wrong, name what was right, take action to correct wrong, remind them to imitate Jesus (1 Corinthians 11:1), and most importantly: "Be on your guard; stand

---

[1] Gary Chapman, Paul White, and Harold Myra, *Rising Above a Toxic Workplace*, (Chicago: Northfield, 2014), 130.

firm in the faith; be courageous; be strong. Do everything in love" (1 Corinthians 16:13–14).

Biblical Advice for Survival

Chapman, White, and Myra provide further advice for surviving toxic workplaces:

- Don't expect people in a toxic workplace to respond 'normally'. Give up your expectation of a healthy response to your good work. Instead, serve the Lord (Colossians 3:23).
- Accept the fact that you cannot change the culture unless you are the leader.
- Set clear boundaries regarding what you will or will not do, and stick to it. Do not lose the person you are 'in Christ' (Romans 8:1), for the sake of pleasing your manager or your company.
- Don't accept false guilt, from those trying to blame others.
- Don't take it personally, remember that toxic culture is an outworking of rampant sin, not your personal responsibility. Pass the burden to Jesus (Matthew 11:28–30).
- Have people who will affirm you, preferably who can give you clear feedback on your working, so that you can evaluate yourself with sober judgement (Romans 12:3).[2]

Leading for a Flourishing Work Culture

While a toxic culture can teach us a lot about the abuse of power and authority, those who do have influence in their organisation need to reverse such strategies to ensure that a healthy and flourishing culture develops.

An organisation in the US surveys to find the "best Christian workplaces" and measure employee engagement and satisfaction. The following list gives us an idea of how we can behave in our own

---

[2] Gary Chapman, Paul White, and Harold Myra, *Rising Above a Toxic Workplace*, (Chicago: Northfield, 2014), 142–143.

organisations, and the sort of Christian culture we can influence around us.

These are Best Christian Workplaces Institute's top survey responses for employee engagement:

- I know what is expected of me at work.
- I am very satisfied with the opportunities I have to use my skills and spiritual gifts in my job.
- I am satisfied with the recognition I receive for doing a good job.
- My supervisor cares about me as a person.
- Someone at work encourages my development.
- My organisation acts on the suggestions of employees.
- The mission and goals of my organisation make me feel my job is important.
- My co-workers are highly committed to excellence in their work.
- I am very satisfied with the level of Christian fellowship and spirituality in my organisation.
- Someone at work talks to me about my progress regularly.
- In the past year, I have had opportunities at work to learn and grow.
- My organisation's leaders behave with fairness and integrity.
- My organisation has a winning strategy for serving our customers/ supporters.
- Employees at my organisation are encouraged to experiment and be innovative.
- My organisation is well managed.[3]

---

[3] *Best Christian Workplaces Institute,* "Building Employee Commitment and Engagement in Christian Organizations", 2007. http://bcwinstitute.org/resources/Press/2007%20Building%20Employee%20Commitment.pdf (cited 18-Dec-2017).

Prayer:

Dear loving Lord,

It is so hard when we see the impact of sin in our workplaces.

We know that you hate sin and the way it can destroy relationships and the fabric of your creation.

Forgive us for any part we might play in fuelling a toxic culture by participating in gossip, humiliation, blame; by not working hard; or by not helping others flourish.

Help us to provide places of refuge for others. Help us to be agents of encouragement and affirmation.

If we are the victims in such situations, then help us to stand firm. Help us to remember who we are in Christ.

Help us to focus on working for you.

Give us the wisdom, and prompt us to know when to leave.

AMEN

Taking It Further:

1

Rate your organisation according to the checklist of a toxic workplace. How does it rate? What needs to improve? How much influence do you have over the things that need to improve?

2

Run through the list of factors for a healthy culture marked by good employee engagement and satisfaction. How many items on that list could you strongly agree with? What needs to be affirmed? What needs to change? Whom can you influence for change?

3

Study 1 and 2 Corinthians further to list toxic elements and Paul's remedies. What can be applied in your situation? What is new that you have discovered?

4

Read Louise's story again. Analyse what she has described according to the material in this chapter. Put together biblical verses that might encourage her in her situation. What are three strategies that you would recommend to her?

Chapter 9
Non-Selfish Ambition

A friend of mine was seeking to recruit a young woman who had worked for a major consulting organisation. She was a wonderful prospect: intelligent, enthusiastic, a great writer, and a strategic thinker. So he decided to do a reference check.

Her former manager was very positive about her, but he did have a concern. "She did not really fit the culture here," he said, "Several times, she passed up the best assignments which might have fast-tracked her career. She seemed to prefer assignments with small not-for-profit organisations. She seemed to exercise a passion for justice and was taking too long to climb the corporate ladder. Frankly, she lacks ambition."

My friend was delighted with the description and subsequently employed the young woman, who has been an outstanding appointment. He saw the accusation of lacking "ambition" as a positive mark of her character — that is, that she lacked *selfish* ambition.

"Monster Ambition"

For Christians, there is often a difficulty living within the modern corporate culture where ambition is seen as a prerequisite for success. In an article widely circulated on LinkedIn, author and CEO Mark Stevens writes about the "Monster Ambition" that employees need to demonstrate in the workplace:

- Achieve goals no matter what it takes
- Step over competition to win
- Forget about balance in your life
- Don't buddy with others in the office[1]

While these behaviours seem extreme, they are reasonably common in corporate culture. But they work against positive work relationships, trust, teamwork, and also impact home life.

---

[1] Mark Stevens, "Why Monster Ambition Wins in the Workplace", *LinkedIn*, 19 August 2014. https://www.linkedin.com/pulse/20140819213852-10136502-why-monster-ambition-wins-in-the-workplace/ (cited 18-Dec-2017).

Ambition versus Outcomes

Damien was working for an airline company and had a tip-off about an issue brewing in a colleague's department. He relayed the information to his colleague, who was shocked.

"Why are you telling me this?" he asked.

"Because we're on the same team," Damien said in surprise.

"No, we're not. We are competing. Don't think I will repay the favour," said his colleague.

That was one of several signals that made Damien realise he could not continue in that organisation. However, he has had major success in several other organisations that **did** value working relationships, teamwork, integrity, and results.

Christian Ambition

I have worked with a woman who is very ambitious, but seeks to express that ambition in a Christian way. Together we reviewed biblical literature and other helpful information to determine how she can use her passion effectively. We concluded that the Bible dismisses selfish ambition, but rewards passion for God and others, even if you benefit through use of that drive.

The Bible gives us a balanced view of self, affirming that the self is made in God's image and likeness, and therefore has God-given value (Genesis 1:27). This includes ambition, since some of us have been created with the gift of ambition. R. Paul Stevens points out that there is value in ambition, since without ambition we would be passive and complacent, lacking direction.[2] For Christians, ambition gives force and passion to seeking God's purposes, and ambitious people are initiators, future-oriented, creative, and consistently motivated.

However, we need to ensure that our passions align with what God cares about. Not everything we do is affirmed by God, since our sinful nature gives us a tendency to be self-centred (2 Timothy 3:2).

---

[2] R. Paul Stevens, "Ambition" in *The Complete Book of Everyday Christianity*. Edited by Robert Banks and R. Paul Stevens (Singapore: Graceworks, 2011).

The Bible refers to the tendency to selfish ambition several times. In Galatians 5:20, Paul uses a Greek word that referred to work done for pay or accepting a position not for service but for what one can get out of it.[3] James declares "selfish ambition" to be a form of earthly, unspiritual, and demonic "wisdom" (James 3:13-16).

There are subtler warnings elsewhere. In Matthew 6:33, Jesus calls his disciples to a life of self-sacrifice, giving priority to God's kingdom and righteousness; and in Luke 14:10–11, he warned against desiring power, prestige, and wealth. In Romans 12:2, Paul warns against being conformed to the mindset of the world, including the focus on ambition. He also speaks out against uncontrolled desires, which may include ambition (Philippians 3:19); and against the love of money, which may be a source of ambition, (1 Timothy 6:10).

Stevens lists several symptoms of selfish ambition, which stands as a useful checklist to evaluate our behaviour. Do we:

- Define our self by our achievements rather than our character?
- Find meaning in our own life rather than as a child of God?
- Relentlessly strive, finding it difficult to rest?
- Get discouraged by a lack of recognition for our hard work?
- Exercise predatory competition, that is, stepping on or over others to achieve what we want?
- Use the present situation as a stepping stone, continually looking at the next thing?[4]

Jesus on Ambition
Rather, we need to follow Jesus' advice by denying ourselves, sacrificing our personal desires (Matthew 16:24), while still having healthy self-esteem, implied in the command to love our neighbours *as* we love ourselves (Matthew 19:19).

---

[3] Note that Paul often refers to his lack of such 'selfish ambition' by detailing how he worked hard to cover his own costs while evangelising (Acts 20:34, 1 Corinthians 9:12, 2 Thessalonians 3:6).
[4] R. Paul Stevens, "Ambition" in *The Complete Book of Everyday Christianity*. Edited by Robert Banks and R. Paul Stevens (Singapore: Graceworks, 2011).

Well-known management consultant Ken Blanchard has described this conundrum neatly: Bad Ego is when we Edge God Out, through either fear or pride; while Good Ego is when we Exalt God Only, with humility and confidence.[5]

As our example let us consider Jesus, who did not lack ambition. He knew he was the Son of God destined to sovereignty. However, he did not boast, take credit, show off or demand attention; nor did he operate from fear by hiding behind his position or withholding information.

Instead, Jesus had a perfect balance of humility and confidence, as Paul points out to the Philippians in 2:3–11: "Do nothing out of selfish ambition or vain conceit. Rather, in humility value others above yourselves, not looking to your own interests… In your relationships with one another, have the same mindset as Christ Jesus: who, being in very nature God, did not consider equality with God something to be used to his own advantage; rather, he made himself nothing by taking the very nature of a servant…"

Jesus was born in a barn, not in a palace; lived an itinerant lifestyle, hand to mouth; and died a shameful death, on a cross. He voluntarily separated himself from God not for his own power or glory, but in obedience and for our sakes. As he said, he came to serve, not to be served (Matthew 10:45).

The ultimate check on our ambition is that we should love God pre-eminently, with our whole self, heart, and soul (Matthew 22:37). If we are continually conscious of God as our audience, then we will be more aware when our words, behaviour, and actions do not meet his standards.

---

[5] Ken Blanchard, *Lead like Jesus* (Nashville: Thomas Nelson, 2008).

Prayer:

Dearest Lord,

We pray with gratitude for those who are ambitious for you and for others.

We ask that you would continue to renew their passion and energy.

Help us to know how to serve others before ourselves in our organisations.

Protect us from the desire to gain at the expense of others, and to be content.

When we are tempted to those behaviours that edge you out, give us the ability to stop and change.

Give us the assurance that you will reward us for our obedience, and courage to entrust our future to you. When we are scared we will miss out, renew our faith that you will provide for us.

Help us to be honest in evaluating ourselves and our actions, and to make the changes that are needed.

AMEN

Taking It Further:

1

Consider the "Monster Ambition" description. List the ways that your organisation upholds or rewards those characteristics. How difficult would it be for you **not** to behave in that way?

2

Work through the checklist of selfish ambition. Answer each question as honestly as you can. If you are willing, allow someone who knows you well to give you feedback on each question. What needs to change? Who will keep you accountable?

3

Consider the story of Joseph (Genesis 37–50), particularly chapters 37 and 50. How did the ambitious young man of Genesis 37 rise to be Prime Minister of Egypt? How did his behaviour toward his brothers and father change between chapters 37 and 50?

4

There is a suggestion in this chapter that selfish ambition is the antithesis of teamwork. Write a 250-word reflection on that, perhaps using the following resource as a thought starter: https://www.institutelm.com/resourceLibrary/how-can-leaders-prevent-ambition-from-mutating-into-aggression.html. Are there times when ambition and teamwork can work together?

Chapter 10

A Biblical Reflection on Unemployment

(Much of the material in this chapter initially appeared on The Gospel Coalition Australia *website[1])*

Recently I went through a very difficult period, when I did not have a job. My contract had not been renewed and I was looking for work for nine months. It was not an easy time. It made me question God: why had he done this to me? It made me question myself: who am I? It led me through a rollercoaster of emotions, and to be fearful of the future.

Having said that, this was also an opportunity to reflect on what I could learn about God, the Bible, and what it means to be unemployed.

I learnt four lessons:

1. We are never without work

Work is one of God's first gifts to humans. We read about it in Genesis 2:15, "The Lord God took the man and put him in the Garden of Eden to work it and take care of it." While it is also subject to the curse in Genesis 3, it is the process of working that is cursed, never work itself. That explains why work is harder than it should be and often a source of frustration. But the fact that work was a good gift from God means that we were created to work.

One of the sad features of modern society is the way work is linked to pay. It means that much valuable work is not recognised or valued as highly, such as parenting, housework, caring for people, helping out at the local school or sporting team, and also the joyful work of praying and praising God. While I was lacking paid work, there was still plenty of meaningful work I was doing.

2. God wants to separate our identity from our work

Ironically, my previous job had focused on the connection

---

[1] "You are never without work (A Biblical reflection on unemployment)", *The Gospel Coalition Australia*, 23 May 2016. https://au.thegospelcoalition.org/article/you-are-never-without-work-a-biblical-reflection-on-unemployment/ (cited 28-Dec-2017).

between faith and work. When people asked me the biggest threat to Christians in the workplace, I always responded: when your identity becomes too closely linked to your work. When I was unemployed, I began to learn about that threat personally. In spite of my best efforts, I had underestimated how much my identity was linked to my role. This is a very common experience in our society. Notice what happens next time someone meets you for the first time. They will very quickly ask you, "What do you do?" Instead of replying with a list of activities, you will usually respond with, "I am..." That is a strong statement of identity. I am a writer and a lecturer. That identity helped me make sense of my place in the world.

However, God wants our identity to be rooted in Christ. Read Ephesians 1 and notice how many times Paul reinforces our identity as being 'in Christ'. This gives us powerful freedom, since we are no longer subject to the power or threats of an employer.

3. God wants us to receive our self-esteem from his love

Another trap for Christians is getting their sense of significance from work. We proudly proclaim our role, and unconsciously measure another's worth both by the importance of their role and how much they are paid. I have a friend who is between significant roles. She was an executive with a major corporation, and now she works in hospitality to pay the bills while she continues to apply for roles. She quickly tired of the looks of confusion and pity from her corporate friends when they learned of her new work. She now describes her role as working for a friend to maximise his success in small business.

Our sense of value should be embedded in the fact that we are made in the image of God, and that he loved us so much that he sent his son Jesus to die for us. When this knowledge becomes lived out it protects us from the feelings of worthlessness so common amongst the unemployed.

4. God wants us to look to him for our security

A third trap is that we depend on our work to make us feel secure in this world. God wants us to depend on him rather than our job, and to look to him for all that we need. God has promised countless times that he will provide for our needs (Psalm 84:11; Matthew 6:32–33; Philippians 4:19).

The temptation is to continually look for more security, in spite of a graphic story Jesus told about the foolishness of such an approach and the fragility of life (Luke 12:13–21). As Jesus warned, our security should lie in our being "rich toward God". I have found great comfort in Proverbs 16:9, that while I might seek to plan the way, it is God who "establishes my steps". Yet often the guiding hand of God becomes obvious only when we look behind us.

The Importance of Church Community

While all of this is head knowledge, the reality is that this was a tough time for me and my family. It was a time when the church community was particularly precious. There I felt welcomed not because of the role I had, or the number of people who admired me, or the size of my pay and bank balance — but because I was a fellow believer in Christ, equally loved by God, sharing in the ultimate security of eternal life. Church was also a source of purposeful work: preaching, praying, caring for others, and being a useful member of the community. Once again, though, we must guard against even our work in the church becoming something we identify with more than who we are in Christ.

The Bible and the church community have a lot of hope to offer to those who are unemployed; and in taking a biblical perspective on unemployment, we might also correct our own idolatrous relationship with work.

Prayer:

To the God who knows us intimately,

We pray for those who are unemployed or are prevented from working by illness, addiction, or government regulations.

We know that everybody needs to work to feel more human, to contribute to society, to fulfil what it means to be made in the image of God the Worker.

Please use this time to help them look to you for their sense of identity, for the basis of their self-esteem, and for their security. Help them to be reassured with who they are and all the riches they have in Christ.

Please guide those people to meaningful work, paid or unpaid.

Help them to find safe havens in their church communities.

AMEN

Taking It Further:

1

List all the different sorts of work you have, paid or unpaid. What gratifies you about this list? What challenges you about this list? What could change?

2

Think of your church's local community. Research how significant the problem of unemployment is in your area. In what ways could your church reach out to those who are struggling with unemployment? E.g. Run a CV-writing workshop; host a weekly social meeting to encourage those who are unemployed; advocate for job opportunities in your local area; create work opportunities at the church — paid or unpaid — for those who want to work; provide food hampers or other forms of tangible support.

3

Look at Ephesians 1 and identify all the blessings we have in Christ. Write these out in your own words and apply them to your everyday world. For example, in verse 1, Paul writes to "the faithful in Christ Jesus". Therefore Jesus is both the source and the object of our faith. This means we can draw on him as our model of faithfulness, and pray to him when we feel our faith failing.

4

Think back to a time when you experienced unemployment. Reflect on what you learned through this time. Write a letter to your "unemployed self" giving encouragement and acknowledging what was endured and what was learnt.

Chapter 11
Women and Work

When I started writing this series on work, I was conscious that not many women are writing in this space. Of those who do, many write about specific female-related issues, especially the need to juggle our roles of mothering and supporting our working husbands alongside our work. They have written extremely well about these issues, and a recent significant addition is Katelyn Beaty's *A Woman's Place*.

I have not wanted to be pigeon-holed as a writer and speaker about women's issues, or find an audience that consists mostly of women. This has subtly happened regardless. I have been intrigued that some of the reviews of my first volume of *Workship* have focused on the devotional aspects of questions and prayers rather than wrestled with the ideas. The frequent comment that goes with introducing me is how unusual it is to have a woman speaking on these issues.

Yet, this is an area which I do feel compelled to speak on. There has been a significant entry of women into the workforce across all occupations since 1970. In the US, the makeup of women in the workforce has grown from approximately 38% to 48%.[1] In Australia, it is an increase from 35% to just over 45%.[2] In Singapore, there has been a focus on those in the 'Nappy Valley' — the child-bearing years— to encourage mothers to return to work. There are government incentives and a recent conference attracted big corporates such as Google, Apple, Amazon, JP Morgan, and Credit Suisse.[3]

However, this movement to work has challenged traditional theological views of a woman's place. Katelyn Beaty explains after her research of more than 120 Christian women:

> The women I spoke to *liked* their work. They all had gifts and aspirations for life beyond getting married, having children,

---

[1] Mehroz Baig, "Women in the Workforce: What Changes Have We Made?", *Huffington Post*, 19 December 2013. https://www.huffingtonpost.com/mehroz-baig/women-in-the-workforce-wh_b_4462455.html (cited 18-Dec-2017).

[2] Greg Jericho, "Changing role of women in the workplace", *ABC News*, 10 October 2012. http://www.abc.net.au/news/2012-10-10/jericho-women-employment/4303454 (cited 18-Dec-2017).

[3] Elaine Lee, "More firms wooing mums back to work", *The New Paper*, 14 August 2017. http://www.tnp.sg/news/singapore/more-firms-wooing-mums-back-work (cited 18-Dec-2017).

and tending a home... For nearly all the women I spoke with, the desire to work came with a lot of *churning*. Very few of the women were fully at peace with work. Sometimes the churning came from within... self-doubting questions... For many women, there was lingering guilt about professional aspirations... And sometimes the churning was stirred up by others... Professional work has also been rolled into larger ideological skirmishes about parenting and what's best for children...

I, too, have experienced churning around work. I have struggled to balance the demands of running a magazine [Beaty was the youngest editor of *Christianity Today*] with the demands of friendship, family and church... I have not always known how to supervise men. I have wondered whether women must choose between pursuing a career or pursuing marriage and family.[4]

There have been disappointing developments in the last couple of years, with a gender role backlash against women's increasing confidence and involvement in the workforce.

In 2015, a woman asked evangelical leader John Piper (author, pastor, founder of *The Gospel Coalition* and *Desiring God* websites) if she could be a Christian, a complementarian[5], and a police officer. In his technical response, Piper talked about the difference between directive and non-directive roles, and personal and non-personal roles. To make it clearer, he gave the example of an army drill sergeant:

For example, a drill sergeant might epitomize directive influence over the privates in the platoon. And it would be hard for me to see how a woman could be a drill sergeant —

[4] Katelyn Beaty, *A Woman's Place* (New York: Howard Books, 2016), 3–5.
[5] Complementarianism is a theological view that men and women are equal but have complementary responsibilities in marriage, family life, and leadership. Typically, the male has 'headship' responsibilities and is preferred in leadership roles over women.

hut two, right face, left face, keep your mouth shut, private —
over men without violating their sense of manhood and her
sense of womanhood.[6]

This extension of the complementarian theology to positions in
society, rather than at home and church, is an unwelcome development.
In 2017, the same issue was raised in the Equip Women's
Conference in Sydney, Australia. As *Eternity News* reported: "One
speaker even said that if a woman became a CEO she should perform
her role in a way that was helpful to men. In a video shown during the
conference, a female minister says what makes her happy is when she
is able to make her male colleagues 'shine,' a point that was taken up at
the end by Equip chair Isobel Lin."[7]

I feel this is poor exegesis of passages in 1 Corinthians 11, 1
Timothy 2, and Ephesians 5, which describe the relationship of women
and men at home and in places of worship, but not in terms of their
roles in society. By contrast, Proverbs 31 has a much more empowering
description of a woman.

The Freedom and Limits of the Proverbs 31 Woman

I know some women groan when Proverbs 31:10-31 is read out,
because it seems like the impossible ideal of a woman. The majority of
conservative scholars treat this passage at face value as a description of
a woman of good character.

Many translations use the word "noble" in verse 10, but "valiant"
is a better translation. We have here a warrior woman. "Bringing food
from afar" in verse 14 has connotations of hunting down prey. In verse
18, her trading is "profitable" not from good luck, but because she has
worked hard. She is brave and strong and industrious and courageous.

---

[6] Limits of space prevent me explaining this more fully, but a transcript of the question and answer
can be found here: https://www.desiringgod.org/interviews/should-women-be-police-officers
(cited 18-Dec-2017).

[7] Anne Lim, "When cutting your hair can be an ungodly act," *Eternity News*, 29 May 2017. https://
www.eternitynews.com.au/culture/when-cutting-your-hair-can-be-an-ungodly-act/ (cited 18-
Dec-2017).

Psalm 111 is a heroic poem about God, yet we see similar characteristics. Just like the wife, the Lord is celebrated amongst the elders. The Lord is gracious and compassionate, provides food, and is faithful, just, and trustworthy.

I want to take three strong affirmations from this Proverbs 31 poem, and comment about what we lack in relation to it.

Affirmation 1: God Loves Women Who Work

We have to be careful about the context of this poem historically and culturally — this was a domestic work situation. The culture was much more integrated than we are today. There was no concept of going out to work for eight hours then coming home. Work, play, and rest all happened in the same area. You might go out to the fields to work, but that tended not to be a very long commute, and you would return for meals.

One thing we do see clearly is that this woman is being celebrated for her working and for all aspects of her working. There is "wife-ing", mothering, caring for the poor, sewing...

But perhaps the most surprising thing is the entrepreneurial activity celebrated here. This woman is involved in commercial transactions involving land, and in trading in markets:

> She considers a field and buys it;
> out of her earnings she plants a vineyard.
> She sets about her work vigorously;
> her arms are strong for her tasks.
> She sees that her trading is profitable,
> and her lamp does not go out at night. (Proverbs 31:16-18)

This is not something we expect in a patriarchal society.

In fact, it *was* something that happened among the wealthier class at that time. Scholars have identified records, especially in Persia, where women were involved in such activities. What is interesting here, though, is that this woman also sews, which was traditionally the activity of a slave. It means that she was not overtly wealthy, or perhaps that she practised humility, one of the qualities of wisdom.

The passage's exalting statement at the end of Proverbs is clearly a sign that God approves of this woman's work — the way she is stewarding her gifts, taking care of her responsibilities, and serving her community.

This chapter actually is a summary of what has been taught about Lady Wisdom in Proverbs, especially in chapters 8-9. Wisdom speaks truly, receives blessing, is just, and fears the Lord. What is described in those chapters were the virtues of wisdom. What is described in chapter 31 is what wisdom looks like in daily practice: working hard, making good business decisions, caring for the poor, looking after your family, and bringing honour to those who love you.

Affirmation 2: God Loves All Work

I love that this woman is so integrated. There is no division between different activities here and what might please God. There is little reference to spiritual or ritual, and yet it is clear that she "fears the Lord" in verse 30. Every activity is done and offered equally as worship.

Our society functions very differently in the way it separates and values the work we do:

- There is women's work and other work
- There is unpaid work and paid work
- Your status as a person is tied to the level of your remuneration

What is more, our churches impose their own hierarchy:

- Gospel work versus secular work
- Ministry versus other work
- Eternal work versus temporal work

What brings her husband honour, and by extension honour to God, is the faithful way the Proverbs 31 woman does her work. She uses all her opportunities, gifts, and skills, from working with wool and flax in verse 13; ensuring there is good food on the table in verses 14-15; making careful financial decisions and working hard to make it happen in verses 16-18; sewing in verses 19, 21-22, and 24; caring for the poor and needy in verse 20; being recognised for her strength and dignity in verse 25; and teaching others wisdom in verse 26.

Notice what happens at the end of the chapter — This woman is esteemed for her work: "Honor her for all that her hands have done, and let her works bring her praise at the city gate" (v. 31).

Affirmation 3: God Calls Us to Multiple Roles
In some ways, this woman represents the universal woman.

- I have seen these verses used to empower stay-at-home mums.
- We notice that this is a woman who is involved in business affairs.
- I have seen these verses used to remind us of our calling to help the poor.

Sometimes, I think we get sucked into thinking we have one great calling that God is drawing us to, and that our role is to guess what that calling is. In truth, I believe we have a calling to many different roles, in private and in public life, and God calls us to honour him in **all** those roles.

- Some of us are married, some are single. God wants you to serve him in either of those roles.
- Some of us have children, some don't. God wants you to serve him regardless, with the opportunities that both situations enable.
- Some of us are employed, some aren't. But we all have energy and talents to put into activities that have the potential to be meaningful, whether it is a piece of art, a letter to an asylum seeker, a strategic plan for a company, the taking of meals to the housebound, or the tending of the most beautiful flower patch in inner-city Sydney.

Warning

I do want to say a word of warning here. We can't have it all, at least not at the same time. We can't do everything this woman was doing. The major contextual pieces that are missing here are domestic help and community living. They had slaves and servants; and the village helped to raise the children! As working women, especially if we have children, there are enormous demands on us, and the reality is that many of us end up not just time poor but soul poor.[8]

> My mum was expected to work until she got married and then to focus on looking after the house, the children, and her husband. She was actually paid a dowry when she resigned from her company to get married.

> I expected to work, drop out kids, put them in childcare, and rush on. However, I fell so in love with my daughter I never wanted anyone else to spend more waking hours with her than I did. My husband never expected to divert from his career path.

> By contrast, my daughter expects that she and her future husband will share as equally as possible the working and child-care roles.

One thing that challenges me in this Proverbs passage is that the Valiant Woman "laughs at the days to come" (v. 25). There is a freedom in this passage — she seems to be working from strength, not from exhaustion, weakness, or desperation. The things she does, she does because she wants to, not because she has to. There is no compulsion.

To Work Like a Proverbs 31 Woman, We Need Three Things

> Firstly, we need **a realistic view of self**. We need to know what we are capable of and what resources we need. Mostly, we need to know when we aren't coping, when there is a disconnect between

---

[8] For a discussion on spiritual practices for busy women, I recommend Anne Winckel's, *Time Poor Soul Rich* (Sydney: Ark House Press, 2015).

what we see needs to be done and what we are capable of doing. I can say that I struggle in this area. I am always too optimistic about what I can achieve, and it is easy for me to hit the wall. I am learning… from harsh experience.

- Secondly, we need **a deep relationship with God.** Even though this is not mentioned in the passage, it is certainly the foundation of the rest of Proverbs. Proverbs 3:5-6 is an example, "Trust in the Lord with all your heart and lean not on your own understanding; in all your ways submit to him, and he will make your paths straight." We need that healthy spiritual dynamic that is the foundation of our strength. Our churches are vital for stimulating and encouraging such a relationship in all the roles we play, including as businesswomen and professionals. It is always a struggle to maintain our God anchor, but being accountable to others — a small group, a friend, or a prayer triplet — can really help.

- Finally, we need **a vision of what God can achieve through us.** This woman has a real sense of purpose. She knows she is doing good work. Can we see the possibilities God has for us? Are we prepared to ask him? I think we need an attitude of partnering with what God is *already* doing in our workplaces, homes, and neighbourhoods. A friend started praying that God would reveal where he was at work in her workplace. Suddenly, a place that had seemed spiritually barren opened up as she began to have conversations and develop relationships around topics of justice, compassion, and spirituality.

Prayer:

Loving Lord,

Thank you for giving women good work to do.

Thank you for enabling women with gifts and abilities to be part of your mission of stewarding the creation, filling the earth, bringing *shalom*, and reconciling all things under Christ.

Guide us as we seek our callings.

Thank you for the example of the Proverbs 31 Valiant Woman, which opens up so many possibilities for good work.

Help women to work hard to honour you and serve others, while enjoying the benefits of using all their gifts, passions, and experience.

Help us to value equally all types of work done by women.

AMEN

Taking It Further:

1

In her book, Katelyn Beaty captures suggestions from her research for practical ways that churches can equip and empower women. Discuss with your church leader how some of these could be applied:

- Highlight different sorts of women's work from the pulpit, instead of just focusing on women as mothers and men as workers.
- Include examples of professional women and their struggles and victories to help normalise the professional roles of women.
- Offer classes on work and vocation for all, but particularly welcome women, since many will self-select out since the predominant church image for women is mothering.
- Have work-related gatherings based on vocational groupings rather than gender roles, and that includes unpaid vocations.
- Host women's Bible studies and activities other than during the daytime mid-week.
- Publicly celebrate the skills and gifts of all workplace Christians, whether or not they are used in the church. Do not stereotype women's roles in church to helping, care-giving, and hospitality.[9]

---

[9] Katelyn Beaty, *A Woman's Place* (New York: Howard Books, 2016), 245–246.

2

Make a list of all the different roles held by you as a woman, or by a key woman in your life (wife, friend, mother, sister). Write about the particular gifts and passions you bring to those roles. Write about how the different roles complement each other.

3

Think of a younger woman in your network whom you could encourage in all the roles in her lives. Write a summary of this chapter, and what you have learned. Pass it on to her with a crafted prayer for her paid and unpaid work.

4

Are there particular issues of justice or gender-related concern in your workplace or church? Women tend to be particularly vulnerable in areas of bullying, harassment, and unequal pay. How might you advocate on behalf of women in those issues?

Chapter 12
The Future of Work

(*Much of the material appeared in* Zadok Perspectives Winter 2018)[1]

I was invited to join a conversation about *Humanizing Work*, by Rev. Dr Andrew Sloane of Morling College. Our goal was to look at the future of work — particularly advances in robotics and automation — working toward fruitful responses from biblical and theological perspectives.

What ensued was a fascinating discussion involving a theologian, a biblical studies lecturer, a CEO coach, an expert in artificial intelligence, an economist, a church leader, and a business leader.

My contribution was in a couple of areas: as a faith and work expert, and as a woman. Some of the scenarios that we outlined for the future of work included the precariousness of work — development of the 'precariat'[2] — and the concept of portfolio careers, which as I observed, is already the lived experience of many women.

In my lifetime I have changed career seven times, held 22 jobs, and now balance two part-time roles, a couple of projects, and my own writing and speaking endeavours. Right now, I am earning less than at anytime in my working life. However, I have the flexibility I love, and am doing work that energises me while avoiding that which used to drain me.

I am impacted by a lack of job security, do not receive much professional development, and have no career plan. What I experience now is the probable shape of the work of the future — casual insecure piecework, where I wear the cost of my development and the risk of ill health.

During the *Humanizing Work* seminar, we each had the chance to share our observations on how work is changing with the rise of technology, shifting economic levers, and globalisation. Following are some of my observations.[3]

---

[1] http://www.ethos.org.au/publications/Subscriptions/Zadok-Perspectives2 (cited 24-Mar-2018).
[2] A term coined by English sociologist Guy Standing.
[3] I am grateful for the research contribution of Clare Inwood to my preparation for the seminar and the observations that follow.

A Changing Definition of 'Work'

Most people would define work as something you are paid to do. Such a definition is very limiting. It excludes the work which is essential for the functioning of our society but remains largely unremunerated, such as care of children and the elderly; voluntary work through charities, churches, and sporting clubs; and the earth care work of gardening.

We do not see such a limiting definition in the Bible. Work is that which you do with purposeful intent, paid or unpaid, seen or unseen. God is interested in all work which might not be valued economically, including prayer, character formation, and worship in everyday life.

As we look to a future where forecasters anticipate insufficient paid work to go around[4], there is a move to decouple work from the payment received. At one extreme is the concept of the universal basic income (UBI): an amount paid to everyone to cover basic needs of food, clothing, and shelter, regardless of the person's employment.

It is an idea promoted by leaders in the Silicon Valley, the source of much of the technology that is anticipated to displace almost 50% of current jobs. It was popularised recently in a Harvard University commencement speech by Facebook founder Mark Zuckerberg, "We should have a society that measures progress not just by economic metrics like GDP, but by how many of us have a role we find meaningful... We should explore ideas like universal basic income, to make sure that everyone has a cushion to try new ideas."[5]

The change of definition of work is welcome, although there are many critics of the UBI who see its potential to create a culture of laziness and entitlement, and stifle innovation and productivity.

---

[4] Oxford University has estimated that 47% of current jobs will be at risk within the next 20 years because of technology advancement. As quoted in *Fortune* magazine: "Why Free Money for Everyone is Silicon Valley's Next Big Idea". http://fortune.com/2017/06/29/universal-basic-income-free-money-silicon-valley/ (cited 27-Dec-2017).

[5] See Fortune article: http://fortune.com/2017/06/29/universal-basic-income-free-money-silicon-valley/ (cited 27-Dec-2017).

Indeed, the Bible recommends that we should all work, that work is good for personal health and the functioning of community, and that it is good to reward work (not necessarily financially).[6]

The Impact on Those Who Are Vulnerable

It is reasonable to assume that the hardship anticipated as a result of the technological revolution will have a proportionally larger impact on those most vulnerable to economic and labour force changes: the disabled, older workers, youth, and women.[7]

A June 2015 report by the Committee for Economic Development of Australia, called *Australia's Future Workforce?* summarises the technological advances and their impact:

> Computers will reshape the labour market in two key ways:
>
> 1. Directly substitute for labour, with a high probability that as much as 40% of jobs in Australia could be replaced by computers within a decade or two; and
> 2. Disrupt the way work is conducted, expanding competition and reducing the costs to consumers, but also reducing the income of workers.

In *The impact of emerging technologies in the workforce of the future*, Telstra Chief Scientist Professor Hugh Bradlow describes how a range of existing technologies, such as cloud services, Big Data, the Internet of Things, artificial intelligence, and robotics are rapidly reaching the point where they will have widespread impact on the economy.[8]

---

[6] This is especially clear in Paul's letters to the Thessalonian churches, where there was a tendency to not work, in anticipating Christ's return. Paul models hard work (1 Thessalonian 2:9), and is critical of those who are slack and do not work (1 Thessalonians 4:12–14). In fact, work is the act of doing good to one another and to all (1 Thessalonians 5:15).

[7] These impacts have been summarised in various reports, including *Willing to Work*, Australian Human Rights Commission, 2016, and *Report Card 2015*, Foundation for Young Australians.

[8] *Australia's Future Workforce?* CEDA, 2015.

Already there is what has been described as a feminisation of poverty. Social and economic factors such as the lack of superannuation/pensions and asset accumulation due to gender inequality unfairly impact on women, who are further disadvantaged by having taken significant time out of the workforce due to caring responsibilities and/or long term casual or unstable employment.

In Australia, almost 45% of women reported that their quality of life worsened after retirement.[9]

It seems that technology advancement is widening the gap between those who can adapt, and those who struggle already.

Globalisation and the Role of Government

One of the issues with technological advancement is that it is outpacing governments' ability to react. Already we have seen it with the transport disruptor Uber. In September 2017 in the UK, Uber was stripped of its London licence years after it had started operating, due to a 'lack of corporate responsibility'.[10] Among the criticisms: the way Uber treats its drivers as 'sweat labourers' with no minimum wage, and a high cost of meeting Uber's vehicle requirements.[11]

A McKinsey Report has indicated that companies such as Uber, Google, Amazon, and Facebook are so globally omnipresent that governments struggle to regulate them. It is increasingly the private sector that is investing and setting policy for technological advancement. It outlines the issues that go beyond geographical boundaries:

> Encouraging broader uptake of technologies to ensure competitive markets.

---

[9] *Doing it Tough*, Wesley Mission Brisbane, 2015.

[10] As reported in *The Guardian*: "Uber stripped of London licence due to lack of corporate responsibility", 22 September 2017. https://www.theguardian.com/technology/2017/sep/22/uber-licence-transport-for-london-tfl (cited 27-Dec-2017).

[11] This was documented in a UK parliamentary enquiry, as reported in *The Guardian*: "Uber is treating its drivers as sweated labour, says report", 9 December 2016. https://www.theguardian.com/technology/2016/dec/09/uber-drivers-report-sweated-labour-minimum-wage (cited 27-Dec-2017).

- Addressing employment and income-distribution concerns.
- Resolving ethical, legal, and regulatory issues.
- Ensuring the availability of data.[12]

Taking up just one of those challenges — ethical issues — the authors of the report outline the following concerns:

> Real-world biases risk being embedded into training data. Since the real world is racist, sexist, and biased in many other ways, real-world data that feeds algorithms will also have these features — and when AI algorithms learn from biased training data, they internalize the biases, exacerbating those problems. There are also concerns about the algorithms themselves — whose ethical guidelines will be encoded into them, what rights should people have to understand the decision-making process, and who will be responsible for their conclusions? This has led to calls for algorithmic transparency and accountability. Privacy is likewise a concern — who should have ownership of data, and what safeguards are needed to protect highly sensitive data, such as health-care data, without destroying its usefulness?[13]

How Can the Church Respond to Future Work Scenarios?

During the industrial revolution, it was Christians who led many of the leading companies. It was the Protestant work ethic that enabled the rise of capitalism. It was Christians at the forefront of the union movement that were involved in tempering the excesses of capitalist endeavour, and it has been the church that has spoken in favour of limiting work hours, improving work conditions, quarantining Sunday as a day off for families to worship, maintaining public holidays, and guaranteeing minimum wages.

---

[12] *Artificial Intelligence: The Next Global Frontier?* McKinsey & Company, June 2017, 36-37.
[13] Ibid, 37.

However, in most western democracies, churches no longer command the same position in the public square. Their influence has been impacted by scandals such as the child abuse epidemic, falling membership, and increasing secularisation of government and society. Notwithstanding our reduced influence, this is an area where we have much to contribute. The Bible provides an ethical framework, a robust understanding of work and the dignity of the worker, and points to a higher authority than governments or CEOs. Also, Christians in most countries still run the charities that deal with the fallout of wage inequality, labour market change, and poverty.

One of the most distinctive features of the 'digital vortex' which we are in is the way it speeds up business and our lives. A study by the Center for Digital Business Transformation in 2015 indicates that businesses and individuals will become hyperaware with 24/7 quick data turnaround, allowing democratisation of decision-making and fast execution via dynamic processes. It is here that the deep rhythms and rituals laid down in the Bible can encourage us to prioritise taking time out, switching off, and pursuing deep wisdom rather than shallow information.[14]

The future of work must be something Christians watch closely and prepare strategies for, to mitigate its dangers, enhance the dignity of our work, and protect the soul of the worker.

---

[14] Jeff Loucks et. al., *Digital Vortex*, (Lausanne: DBT Center Press, 2016), 180.

Prayer:

To the Lord who is sovereign over time and history,

Thank you for the wonders of technology that enables much good work.

Thank you for the innovation that flows, and the empowerment that many experience.

We are also conscious that there can be a dark side to the rampant development in robotics, engineering, and disruptive technologies.

We pray now for wisdom in dealing with the repercussions, particularly with the possible impact on vulnerable people.

We are also concerned about the ethical frameworks that need to be applied, and the government policy settings that should be in place.

Empower Christians to influence through organisations and government positions, and in public debates.

Help us to be a voice for the voiceless, to love mercy, act justly, and walk humbly.

AMEN

Taking It Further:

1

What is your experience of precarious work — work that is casual, unstable or poorly paid? What was your sense of identity, esteem, and security during that experience?

2

What are the implications of a change in the definition of work? Who could be empowered? Do some research and list the pros and cons of the universal basic income. Study the relevant verses in 1 and 2 Thessalonians. What would Paul recommend?

3

Who are the vulnerable in your community who might be impacted by changes in technology? Which organisations could act to offset the impact? How is your church and congregation members positioned to respond to the challenges of such change?

4

Deloitte have published some responses for leaders to the future challenges of work; see https://www2.deloitte.com/us/en/pages/human-capital/articles/transitioning-to-the-future-of-work-and-the-workplace.html. Reflect on how Christian leaders can respond to these challenges. What does this mean for the way that churches might be organised or led? Where are the opportunities for churches and Christians to influence our culture and society?

Introduction to Section 2:
Helping Churches to Equip Workplace Christians

I have observed a movement in churches from an attractional model, where the focus was on the congregation inviting non-believers to events held at the church, hoping they would "catch" the gospel; to the missional model where the church sees itself as the church *gathered* on Sunday, and the church *scattered* Monday to Saturday, with congregation members taking the gospel with them wherever they are.

There are some other models for churches, including churches like CrossLife on the Gold Coast of Australia, which has partnered with a major developer, Stockland, to design and run a community centre for a residential and shopping development. The lead pastor of CrossLife, Matt Hunt, reports that the community accepts that it is appropriate for the church to run their community centre, with a 97% approval rating. Through the coffee shop and childcare centre, CrossLife has contact with 450 non-Christian families throughout the week.[1]

There are also many church plants looking to work more closely with their community's workplaces and leisure centres — especially sporting centres, restaurants, and galleries — to be a gospel presence.

Many great cathedrals around the world have discovered a renewal in identity and purpose. Recognising their position as the hub of their city environments, they now seek ways to connect with the CBD workers and workplaces, to bring new life to the city.

All these newer models require church leaders to find ways to equip their workplace Christians, as well as to challenge themselves in reaching out to their neighbourhood workplaces.

---

[1] Personal interview with the author on 24 February 2016.

In an article in *Leadership Journal* in February 2014, Tom Nelson wrote that he had confessed to his congregation:

Against a backdrop of pindrop silence, I asked the congregation I served to forgive me. Not for sexual impropriety or financial misconduct, but for pastoral malpractice. I confessed I had spent the minority of my time equipping them for what they were called to do for the majority of their week.

I wanted to confess that because of my stunted theology, individual parishioners in my congregation were hindered in their spiritual formation, and ill-equipped in their God-given vocations. Our collective mission had suffered as well. I had failed to see, from Genesis to Revelation, the high importance of vocation and the vital connections between faith, work, and economics. Somehow I had missed how the gospel speaks into every nook and cranny of life, connecting Sunday worship with Monday work in a seamless fabric of Holy Spirit-empowered faithfulness.[2]

These sentiments are echoed in a book by Business as Mission guru Mike Baer, himself a pastor and a businessman. In *The Pastor and the Business Person,* he speaks directly to church leaders:

Pastor, you probably already see the problem. You desire to see your congregation grow and to see your members meaningfully connected in some way to what God is doing in your community and in the world. But you also stand there and watch helplessly as many of your most gifted members drift away to who-knows-what or to ministries outside your church.

How will you respond? Will you condemn them and thus drive the final nail in the coffin? Will you slink away in

---

[2] Tom Nelson, "Who's Serving Whom?", *Leadership Journal* (February 2014).

discouragement? Or will you courageously face the reality that we have done a very poor job of ministering to the business people in our congregation and have failed to engage them in meaningful work for Christ and deal with it?[3]

This is the challenge for all church leaders — the task of equipping their congregations well for the work they do throughout the week, paid or unpaid.

In this section we will first look at specific equipping activities within *church services*:

- Sermons
- Church services
- Interviews

Secondly, at equipping activities within *church communities*:

- Visiting workers
- Training workplace Christians
- Mentoring workers

Finally, equipping activities *beyond* the church walls:

- Chaplaincy in the workplace
- Church presence in the workplace

I hope that through these ideas, churches will be encouraged to follow Tom Nelson's lead in transforming the focus of his church, and will also reap the rewards:

We are still learning and unlearning as we go, doing our best to navigate what it means to narrow the Sunday to Monday

---

[3] Michael R. Baer, *The Pastor and the Business Person* (CreateSpace, 2017).

gap. But I'm encouraged when I receive an email from a CEO or a stay-at-home mum or a student or a retiree in my congregation who now see their Monday lives through the transforming lens of a biblical theology of vocation. I find increasing joy in seeing congregants embrace their paid and non-paid work as an offering to God and a contribution to the common good. Many of my parishioners have a bounce in their step and a new excitement about all of life. For them, the gospel has become coherent and more compelling. They look forward to sharing it with others in various vocational settings and spheres of influence throughout the week.[4]

---

[4] Nelson has since started a pastor network called Made to Flourish (https://www.madetoflourish. org/), aimed at "providing resources and training to empower a growing network of pastors to connect Sunday faith to Monday work for their churches".

Chapter 13

Sermons to Equip
Workplace Christians

It happened again. Here was another sermon where I, as a workplace Christian, got the message that what I do is not good enough.

The text was Genesis 12:1–9, Abraham's calling. From my reading of the passage, Abraham, a farmer, was asked to become a nomadic farmer, "The LORD had said to Abram, 'Go from your country, your people and your father's household to the land I will show you'" (Genesis 12:1). He was made some promises that were not ultimately fulfilled in his lifetime.

The key element (as is picked up in Romans 4 and Hebrews 11) was that Abraham believed God, stayed in relationship with him, and went about his daily toil in obedience and faith. In fact, he was so close to God in all his trust and obedience, that he is described twice in Scripture as God's friend (Isaiah 41:8 and James 2:23).

Somehow, in the sermon that Sunday, Abraham's actions were compared to a missionary's, even when the preacher admitted that Abraham was given no message to speak.

In this way, the hierarchy of Christian vocations was again subtly presented. We were all challenged to give up our 'worthless' secular jobs to do a far greater thing. Of course, the worthlessness of our secular jobs was only implied by the offer of the glittering prize of 'true' Christian service.

For me, the better application was about doing what we are called to do, in obedience to God. Like Abraham it might be farming, or it could be teaching, or policy advising, or running a business, or being a tradesman. The important thing is to walk closely with God in it, be obedient to him, and proclaim our godly inheritance in the way we do what we are gifted to do.

Instead, I felt deflated, conscious that in the eyes of my pastor, who is my teacher and spiritual adviser, I will not be honoured until I stop doing what I feel called and gifted to do, and do something **he** feels called and gifted to do.

True Teaching about Work and Our Spiritual Life
This is the challenge of those sitting in our church pews. How do

we discern the truth of the Bible about working, when much of the teaching seems very skewed?

Nonetheless, there are many church leaders who are trying to do something different, trying to encourage the workers in their congregations. But they are not sure how to do it.

Scott Gibson has identified some of the problems preachers have about preaching on work:

- It is hard for the world of the church to connect with the world of work.
- It is necessary for the preacher to interpret the congregation as well as the passage, since one cannot apply a text unless one understands the context for the audience.
- Preachers and workers have often lived different lives, and preachers lack confidence in speaking to a successful worker.
- Preachers and workers have different priorities: building the church versus sustaining the world.
- Integrating faith and work is extremely difficult.[1]

I occasionally run workshops on "Taking your church to work". They challenge people to think through some of the blocks to communicating a good theology of work, help them to integrate their faith and working, and illustrate ways they can be more intentional for God in their workplaces.

In these workshops, I get a church pastoral team to go out with members of their congregation and spend a minimum of four hours at their workplaces. Then we welcome them back to debrief the experience.

What You Say and What We Hear

The first thing I challenge people about is language. How do we subtly emphasise the sacred-secular divide and make people feel that

---

[1] In "Preaching Today", *Mockler Memo*, No.10, September 2014.

their jobs are inferior? One way is to exhort 'ministry' and downplay ordinary 'work'. I once told a group of theology students that I thought it better if more church leaders viewed their ministry as 'work' and workers in the congregation viewed their work as 'ministry'. There was a very vocal debate about the special concept of ministry and how it should not be diluted. Yet 'ministry' means 'service'.

Mark Greene from the London Institute of Contemporary Christianity talks about the teacher who was brought out the front and commissioned for the 45 minutes a week she spends teaching Sunday School, because it is 'ministry', but is never honoured or prayed for the 40 hours a week she works as a teacher in a much more challenging context.

We need to be careful of the message we give in terms of working, that if we are not prepared to 'go' as a missionary, Bible teacher, or Christian aid worker, then we should 'send'. This gives the message that our secular jobs should be sacrificed as worthless or milked for their money, rather than seen as a potential place of faith expression and creativity.

There is often a portrayal of work as an evil thing. It is commonly linked to greed or idolatry (over-work/ambition/careerism), or blamed for stopping us from prioritising the important, that is, our voluntary church roles.

Will Messenger quotes a businessperson:

My pastor always talks about profit as if it were greed. Well, that shows they know nothing at all about how the business world works. So when the pastor preaches sermons on this, he always tells me to do things that are useless in terms of the value I provide to society. If I started doing the things my pastor suggests, it would ruin my business, and then I couldn't provide jobs, good service for customers, and useful products, so the function I'm filling in society would cease to exist.[2]

---

[2] Chris R. Armstrong, "How the church marginalizes itself from work", *In Trust* (New Year 2013), 20-23.

Preach on Work

I had worked with an Anglican church to devise a sermon series on work titled, "God at Work". It ended up being one of the most popular series they had run. They made an advertising board which read "God at Work" and looked like a building site sign. Some people walked in off the street because they were captivated by the idea of a church talking about work.

The topics of the series were engaging:

Leading Questions	Theme	Application	Text
Work: a necessary evil, or the gift of God?	Design (Steward-ship)	Work & God	Gen 2:15–25 1 Cor 3: 6–15
"What do you do"? — is that the same as, "Who you are"?	Dignity (Identity)	Work & Worth *When do I stand up for what I believe?*	Luke 15:1–7 Luke 16:1–15
Are you just working for the weekend?	Purpose (Integrity & Relation-ships)	Work & Stress *Am I responding as a Christian to my workplace issues?*	Eccl 2:17–25 Col 3:17–4:1 (Ref. Eph 6:5–9)
Since when did 9 to 5 become 24/7?	Pattern (Priorities at Work)	Work & Home *Are my work priorities aligned with my home priorities?*	Isa 55:1–3. Mat 11:25–30
Who are you really working for?	Redemp-tion (Witness)	Work & Faith *How am I dealing with people?*	Genesis 39:1–10 Luke 19:1–10
Work hard — Play hard?	Sabbath (Obedience / Trust)	Work & Rest *Do I have confidence in God's provision?*	Ex 16:4–30 Ex 20:1 & 2, 9–11

What are you really working for?	Creation & Cultivation (Rewards)	Work & Fruitfulness *What am I expecting to get out of my work?*	Gen 3:1–20. Mat 20:1–16
A job worth doing	Service	Work & Others *What is the value of my work?*	Isa 61:1–7. 1Cor 15:50–58

While this was clearly an impressive series, I think it was the *process* of designing the services that was the clue to its popularity. Like most ministers, Steve was unsure of his footing when it came to talking about work, so he formed an advisory group to help him plan. He made sure they incorporated lots of testimonies, interviews, and other input from workers. He also asked them to help him pick out the main points of application.

Becoming More Familiar with the Workplace

David Miller has made the following suggestions for preachers to become more comfortable in dealing with faith and work issues:

- Be present in the work sphere and listen carefully.
- Become workplace literate (e.g. reading the business section of news websites).
- Preach directly to work concerns.
- Use adult education, small groups, and retreats to address workers' sense of work-faith disjunction.
- Train laity in devotional disciplines linked to their work and daily lives.[3]

The most effective way to become more familiar with the place where the majority of your congregation spend most of their lives, is to visit them. This will be treated more fully in a separate chapter, but

---

[3] Chris R. Armstrong, "How the church marginalizes itself from work", *In Trust* (New Year 2013), 20-23.

it is a great way of collecting meaningful work illustrations for your sermons.

Another way of preaching more effectively for the workplace is to workshop your sermon a couple of weeks ahead with a variety of people in the congregation. This is something Tim Keller does. Get a group of people with different frontlines (work, home, community, not-for-profit) and ask them what the Bible passage means in their context.

When you preach you need to be thinking: how can my audience apply this on Monday? If you are unsure how to answer that question, then pose the question to them during the sermon, and ask them to discuss it in small groups.

Prayer:

To the God of truth,

Thank you for the privilege of taking your Word and sharing it with others.

Thank you for the gift of preaching.

Thank you for the opportunity of challenging people about the way they respond to your Word in different contexts.

Help us to be open to learning about the variety of frontlines in our congregations.

Help us to know how we can encourage, support, affirm, and equip people for their ministries.

Make us more aware of the subtle ways we undermine your truth, especially when we elevate the role of preachers and other church workers.

Teach us to be humble and properly understand all we can learn from your Word.

Thank you for the example of Jesus and the way he was a storyteller teaching wisdom that was grounded in everyday life of work and relationships.

Help us to go and do likewise.

AMEN

Taking It Further:

1

If you are a church leader or preacher, check through your last few sermons. If you are a church member, write notes about the sermons you are hearing. How much of the language might alienate workers? How many illustrations relate to workplaces/frontlines? How much of the application dealt with what people do on Mondays?

2

Look at the sermon topic list in the "God at Work" series listed above. Which topic would you like to hear? Which of those topics have you heard sermons on? How appropriate are the Bible passages used?

3

Do some further study on Abraham's story (especially Genesis 12–15). How would you describe his working situation and the choices he made? What were his challenges as a Christian in the marketplace?

4

Write out a plan about the ways you as a church leader can become more familiar with the workplace. Which of the ideas can you put into practice? If you are a church member, invite your pastor or minister to join you at your frontline/in your workplace for a few hours. Discuss with them possible applications from their most recent sermon.

Chapter 14
Church Services

I was in a church service preaching on work, and I noticed that a lot of thought had been put into all the other elements of the service. For one thing, the table out the front was actually modelled after a carpenter's bench, complete with a vice for holding blocks of wood.

The songs and hymns had been carefully chosen to complement the theme. There was a time when it was hard to choose appropriate 'work' songs, but there are an increasing number of resources available and I was introduced to a few that morning.

The prayers were beautifully composed, examining different facets of working — paid and unpaid. They were inclusive and felt very real, touching on challenges and opportunities in various workplaces.

After the prayers, someone stood up and explained that she had been given a word of knowledge. She spoke to 'someone' in the congregation who was suffering from an anxiety about 'taking God to the workplace', but the encouragement was that God was already there. Instead this person was invited to cooperate with God and work together with him in the workplace. Afterwards there was a general prayer that God would help us to be sensitive to his presence in our workplaces.

At the end of the service, the pastor invited everyone to face the nearest exit. Together, we read a benediction encouraging us to be Jesus' eyes, hands, and feet wherever he placed us that week, and to seek to glorify him in everything we thought and did.

I went out enthusiastic for the week ahead, feeling spiritually nourished and prepared.

The Weekly Church Service as Preparation for Mission

The weekly gathering of the church is the appropriate time of preparation for the scattering of the church Monday to Friday. Our worship of God in church should easily be translated to worship of God outside church.

There are simple ways that church services can help those present to reflect on their working for him during the rest of the week.

Setting up the church

Depending on your ability to influence the church space, it could be good to display written testimonials from people, photos of congregation members in their workplaces, artefacts from different vocations, resources for connecting faith and work, or motivational posters (e.g. 'God at Work', 'Work and Worship', Colossians 3:17).

Leading the service

All our church services should be a combination of glorifying God, encouraging one another, and being prepared to do his missional work. A service leader can take us through those different movements of worship, fellowship, and sending out (Upward, inward, outward).

Some simple phrases can help people connect their faith and work:

- "Let's pause to consider how we were open to God this week in our workplace or neighbourhood."
- "Take a minute to tell the person next to you one magic (good thing) or one tragic (difficult thing) from your working this week."
- "As we sing this next song, I want us to think of one thing we are grateful to God for in our working this week."

Being led in a reflection from your own working will help others to learn to look for God's handprints in their own working experiences. For pastors, this may be as simple as thinking of ways your own work intersects with those in the congregation: lots of meetings, running late, skipping lunch, balancing work and family pressures, being on-call 24/7, managing a diverse team, event planning, dealing with email overload, having too many deadlines, project management, experiencing a breakthrough, coping in an open office, etc.

Songs/hymns

There are an increasing number of songs that help us to be aware of our working and everyday world. The following are collated from the

New Zealand *faith@work* website[1], David Welbourn's magnificent collection from *Work in Worship*[2], and *Making Mondays Meaningful* by the Center for Faith & Work and The High Calling[3]. Below are several examples.

"God of Concrete, God of Steel"
(by Richard Granville Jones)
Lord of science, Lord of art,
God of map and graph and chart,
Lord of physics and research,
Word of Bible, faith of Church,
Lord of sequence and design,
All the world of truth is thine.[4]

"God of Offices and Kitchens"
(Australian hymn modified by Colin Wood, to the tune of "What a Friend We Have in Jesus")
God of offices and kitchens
Lecture halls and factory floor,
God of internet, computers,
T.V. screens and so much more.
You are always here around us
Even when we do not know.
Help us realise your presence
That our Spirit life may grow.

"All Who Love and Serve Your City"
(by Erik Routley)

---

[1] *faith@work*, http://www.faithatwork.org.nz/, especially *Resources for churches (Cited 28-Dec-2017).*
[2] "Worship Resources", *Theology of Work Project*, https://www.theologyofwork.org/resources/worship (Cited 28-Dec-2017).
[3] "Making Mondays Meaningful", *Center for Faith & Work*, http://centerforfaithandwork.com/article/make-mondays-meaningful-free-curriculum (Cited 28-Dec-2017).
[4] Copyright © 1968 Stainer & Bell Ltd. All rights reserved. Permission was sought but no response was received.

All who love and serve your city,
All who bear its daily stress,
All who cry for peace and justice,
All who curse and all who bless.

In your day of loss and sorrow,
In your day of helpless strife,
Honour, peace and love retreating,
Seek the Lord, who is your life.[5]

"Before You I Kneel (The Worker's Prayer)"
(by Keith Getty, Kristyn Getty, Jeff Taylor, and Stuart Townend)
Before you I kneel, my Master and Maker,
To offer the work of my hands.
For this is the day you've given your servant;
I will rejoice and be glad
For the strength I have to live and breathe,
For each skill your grace has given me,
For the needs and opportunities
That will glorify your great name.[6]

"Take My Life and Let It Be"
(by Frances Ridley Havergal)
Take my life and let it be
Consecrated Lord to thee
Take my hands and let them move
At the impulse of Thy love

"Everything"
(by Tim Hughes)

God in my resting
There in my working
God in my thinking
God in my speaking [7]

I also commend The Porter's Gate Worship Project, with their album "Work Songs". In 2017, The Porter's Gate hosted an innovative project in New York City to rejuvenate church music around important cultural themes. For two days, 60 songwriters, musicians, scholars, pastors, and music industry professionals from various worship traditions and cultural backgrounds gathered for meaningful conversation about worship and vocation. They then collaborated to create worship that gave language to and affirms the work of the people. The music is contemporary, variable in style, and rich in musicality and work imagery. It is available to download or stream from here: https://theportersgate.bandcamp.com/releases.

Psalms

Psalm 8: Human beings have a special destiny and responsibility as stewards of creation.

Psalm 15: The person of integrity is acceptable to God.

Psalm 19: God's creation bears witness to God's design and plan for the world.

Psalm 46: In times of trouble, God is our strength and support.

Psalm 65: God has ordered the world and given human beings enough to supply their needs.

Psalm 67: God has blessed humankind.

Psalm 90: God sees how human beings have misused his creation.

Psalms 95–96: Thanksgiving to God for his creation and salvation.

Psalm 100: What God has done is cause for rejoicing.

Psalm 104:1–25: Praise to God for the vastness of his creation and the

---

glory of his works.

Psalm 107:23–32: God is active in his creation.[8]

Prayers

There are many collections of prayers and litanies for the workplace listed at the end of this chapter. Below is a series of biblically-focused prayers under common headings, available from The Center for Faith & Work at LeTourneau University.[9]

Lord, we long to worship you together and pray that...

- You would tear down any mental wall dividing the secular from the sacred in our lives and help us recognise that there is not one part of our existence, including our work, about which you do not cry out, "This is mine. It belongs to me" (Psalm 24:1).
- You would help us bring every part of our work before you as an offering of praise and worship, recognising that everything we do is holy to you (Colossians 3:22).
- You would help us do excellent work as an offering to you, because it's what you deserve (Colossians 3:23).

Lord, we long to know and live your Word and ask that...

- We would find wisdom from your Word so that we can live your truth in our workplaces (2 Timothy 3:16–17).
- We would experience "rest" in our labor knowing that you, Lord, are at work in, through, and for us (Psalm 127:2).
- We would find our calling and pursue it with passion (Ephesians 2:10).
- Our work would adorn your doctrine in every respect (Titus 2:10).

---

[8] Available from David Welbourn's *Work in Worship* resource (1997), 105: https://www.theologyofwork.org/uploads/general/WorkInWorshipWelbourn.pdf (cited 18-Dec-2017).

[9] "How to Pray for Your Workplace", *Center for Faith & Work*, http://centerforfaithandwork.com/article/how-pray-your-workplace (cited 18-Dec-2017).

- We who are employers would treat our employees righteously and fairly (Colossians 4:1).
- We would turn from pride, arrogance, self-righteousness, greed, and materialism in order to pursue humility, righteousness, and service to our fellow man at work (Micah 6:8).

Lord, we long to pray boldly and dependently and desire that...
- Prayer would be the evident and controlling force in our work and our place of worship (Colossians 4:2).
- You would provide good work for those of us who are unemployed (1 Thessalonians 4:11–12).
- You would establish and prosper the work of our hands (Deuteronomy 30:9; Psalm 90:17).

Lord, we long to hear stories of rescue and redemption and pray that...
- We would recognise the incredible opportunity that we have to bring the gospel to the people with whom we work (Colossians 4:5–6).
- We would be wise, winsome, gracious, and intentionally influential with non-Christian coworkers (Colossians 4:5–6).
- You would use us to draw coworkers to Christ.

Lord, we long to see your will done on earth as it is in heaven and ask that...
- We would recognise that all prosperity comes from you, Lord, and desire to use it for your glory, not personal ease (Deuteronomy 8:18).
- We who are business leaders would recognise and use our business resources, influence, and capital to the benefit of the citizens of our world with less opportunity (Jeremiah 29:7).

Workplace affirmation and confession prayers:
Lord, we affirm that...

- You are the Lord of the workplace as well as the place of worship, and we owe complete allegiance to you in all places.
- All work that meets legitimate needs is your work to be done in your way and for your glory.
- Prosperity comes from you and is a gift to be used for your glory, not our ease.
- While you made all things for us to enjoy, true satisfaction comes only from you.

Lord, we confess...

- At times we have been proud and arrogant about success, thinking it was because we were smarter, better, worked harder, or deserved your blessing more than others.
- We have sometimes placed success above integrity and power above people. In this we have sinned against You.
- We have often let our love of safety and prosperity quench our courage and compassion.
- We have kept you at a safe distance, mentally locking in the church building away from our daily affairs.
- How much more we could have used your strength, guidance, wisdom, and love if we had only known you are as real a part of our lives on Monday as you are on Sunday.

Lord, we ask that...

- We, as your people, would live ethically distinctive lives, both in public and private.
- We would practise the discipline of craftsmanship in our field, working with all our hearts as if you were our employer, client, or customer we serve — because you are.
- We would pursue what we are gifted to do, finding the

delight and joy of doing the work for which you created us.

🌒 We would be highly intentional about our spiritual influence, being wise, winsome witnesses in our place of work.

🌒 Others would see the reality of your presence in our lives and be attracted to you.

Benediction/sending out

We have been the Church Gathered.
We are now the Church Dispersed.
Remember: Wherever you go, Christ Goes
Whatever you do, Christ Does.
If someone asks what your church is like,
tell them, 'I am what my church is like.'
If someone asks what your church does,
tell them, 'My church does what I do.'
Remember, You may well be the only authentic contact
someone has with Jesus Christ
because they will not come to church,
but you can bring the church to them.
(Rev. Richard Halverson — US Senate Chaplain)[10]

You are God's Servants
gifted with dreams and visions.
Upon you rests the grace of God
like flames of fire.
Love and serve the Lord
in the strength of the Spirit.
May the deep peace of Christ be with you,
the strong arms of God sustain you,

---

[10] "Prayers & Liturgy", *faith@work*. http://www.faithatwork.org.nz/prayers-liturgy/ (cited 26-Feb-2018).

and the power of the Holy Spirit strengthen you in every way.
Amen.

(Diane Karray Tripp)[11]

May the love of God sustain us in our working
May the light of Jesus radiate our thinking and speaking
May the power of the Spirit penetrate all our deliberating
And may all that is done witness to your presence in our lives.
(Rosemary Wass)[12]

---

[11] "Prayers & Liturgy", *faith@work*. http://www.faithatwork.org.nz/prayers-liturgy/ (cited 26-Feb-2018).

[12] Quoted by Alistair Mackenzie in "The Equipping Church" on *Theology of Work Project*, https://www.theologyofwork.org/key-topics/the-equipping-church (cited 26-Feb-2018).

Prayer:

To the God of our Sunday gatherings,

Help us to be mindful of the purpose of our gathering —

To glorify you, to encourage each other, and to prepare one another for our scattering Monday to Saturday.

Help us to bring the outside into our churches, mindful of the everyday.

Increase in us an awareness of you, your love for our work, and your love for those we work among.

Shape in us the ability to do good work that glorifies you and sustains your creation and helps establish your kingdom.

AMEN

Taking It Further:

1

Review your most recent church service outline. How worker-friendly is it? How easy would it be to incorporate some of the elements listed above? Who might struggle with such an approach? What conversations and processes would need to take place?

2

Have a look at the website resources listed in the chapter and below, and collect further ideas for incorporation into your church services.

3

Review the psalms listed, and the verses used for prayers. Are you comfortable with the interpretation used in the psalm summary and prayers? Are there more appropriate verses, psalms, or themes to use for work-centred prayers?

4

Have a focus group of people in your church from a variety of working situations (fulltime, part-time, casual, paid, unpaid, volunteer), and ask them for ideas about incorporating their Monday–Saturday concerns into the church service. Test some of the ideas listed above. Get some feedback on the ways the church service can be more effective in equipping workers.

Websites for other resources (cited on 19 December, 2017):
- Industrial Christian Fellowship (UK): http://www.icf-online.org/icfprayers.php
- London Institute for Contemporary Christianity: https://www.licc.org.uk/resources/ (Click on *Explore*, and select *Church*)

- Theology of Work Project, "The Equipping Church Overview": A collection of great ideas from Alistair Mackenzie: https://www.theologyofwork.org/key-topics/the-equipping-church
- A litany for the affirmation of human work from the Episcopal Church, US: http://arc.episcopalchurch.org/ministry/dailylife/mdl0407.htm
- A litany for the Labour Day Weekend (Evangelical Lutheran Church US): http://www.liturgybytlw.com/Pentecost/Labor.html

Chapter 15

Interviews with Workers

R. Paul Stevens has been involved in the faith and work space before it was even remotely popular. His book, initially called *Abolition of the Laity* and renamed *The Other Six Days*, argued strongly for the priesthood of all believers, with all the consequences that flow from that understanding, such as honouring the work that people do.

He has lectured at Regent College in Vancouver for almost 30 years on equipping the whole people of God for leadership, everyday spirituality, spirituality and work, theology of work, and marketplace theology.

His magnum opus is a compilation with Robert Banks called *The Complete Book of Everyday Christianity* (recently republished by Graceworks). It covers many aspects of working, including business ethics, calling, management, office politics, part-time employment, shiftwork, and workplace stress.

When asked to name the one thing he would insist on changing in the church's culture for supporting Christians at work, Stevens replies:

> "Give me three minutes and four questions in a service every Sunday for a year. I would get a different person up in front of the congregation each week and ask them:
> 1. Tell us about the work you do.
> 2. What are some of the issues you face in your work?
> 3. Does your faith make a difference to how you deal with these issues?
> 4. How would you like us to pray for you and your ministry in the workplace?
> 5. Then we would pray for them."[1]

All of Life Interviews

A pastor who has experienced the transformative impact of interviews of workers is Jim Mullins from Redemption Church in Arizona. He

---

[1] Quoted by Alistair Mackenzie in his article "The Equipping Church" in the *Theology of Work Project*. https://www.theologyofwork.org/key-topics/the-equipping-church (cited 19 December 2017).

reports that, over time, "These interviews have slowly helped all of us to understand that 'vocation is integral, not incidental, to the mission of God in the world,' as Steve Garber says. We have noticed increased theological depth and gospel intentionality in our congregants and their work. This is the work of the Spirit, but we are delighted that he is using the interviews as an instrument of his grace."

Jim calls his interviews "All of Life Interviews", and has a slightly different set of questions from Stevens', which he explains below:

Question #1: How would you describe your work?
"We want a snapshot of the daily life of the interviewee. This answer often builds common ground between the interviewee and others within the congregation, even if they don't work in the same field."

Question #2: As an image-bearer of God, how does your work reflect some aspect of God's work? (Genesis 1:26-28; 1 Corinthians 10:31; Ephesians 5:1; Colossians 3:17)
"We want to ground the intrinsic value of work in the character of God and frame our work as an act of 'image-bearing' (Genesis 1:16–28; 2:15). Therefore, we ask the interviewees to connect their work to some specific aspect of God's work."

Question #3: How does your work give you a unique vantage point into the brokenness of the world? (Genesis 3; Romans 3:10–20)
"Some people subconsciously think their work should always be fun and fulfilling, often assuming that the presence of pain and struggle invalidates the goodness of their work. We want them to see that, in a fallen world that is filled with sin and its effects, each occupation has unique hardships and comes with its own thorns and thistles."

Question #4: Jesus commands us to "love our neighbours as ourselves." How does your work function as an opportunity to love and serve others? (Mark 10:35–45; Ephesians 5:1; Romans 12:14–21; Colossians 1:24–27)

"We want to broaden the application of Jesus' command to love our neighbours. Many people assume this command is mostly applied as interpersonal acts of kindness, but we try to demonstrate that love can also be indirect and systemic."[2]

This Time Tomorrow

Mark Greene has long promoted a segment called "TTT = This Time Tomorrow". The questions are very simple:

- Where will you be this time tomorrow?
- What do you do there?
- What are your challenges and joys?
- How can we pray for you?

A sample of such an interview can be found here: https://www.youtube.com/watch?v=PztfPLTX5VE&feature=youtu.be.

Matthew Waldron, pastor at Three Crosses Church in Perth, Australia, has produced some resources to use TTT in a congregational setting and at Sunday School. The materials, reproduced in Appendix 1, include advice for congregation members who are asked to participate. Green summarises the following benefits:[3]

1. It acknowledges, affirms, and honours the interviewee, telling them that what they do every day is important to the leader, important to the church, and important to God.

---

[2] Jim Mullins, "The Butcher, the Baker, and the Biotech Maker", *The Gospel Coalition*, 29 October 2014. https://www.thegospelcoalition.org/article/the-butcher-the-baker-and-the-biotech-maker (cited 26-Feb-2018).

[3] See "This Time Tomorrow", *The London Institute for Contemporary Christianity*, 28 February 2017. https://www.licc.org.uk/resources/this-time-tomorrow/ (cited 26-Feb-2018).

2. As TTT follows TTT month by month, the whole congregation recognises ever more deeply that ordinary Christians doing ordinary things are important to God — even if some people never get to share from the front.
3. TTT creates new conversations. It gives people who didn't know the interviewee an easy way to talk to them, and perhaps to share similar challenges and pertinent insight or encouragement.
4. TTT triggers a new kind of conversation. Issues that are often considered inappropriate for church — work, futility, failure, success, daily relationships, mission in daily life — are validated as legitimate topics for conversation.

Whom to Interview

It may be tempting to focus on those in positions of authority and power, but it is much more effective to celebrate the stories of ordinary people in everyday work as well.

Try to get a diversification of vocations, positions of authority, genders, cultures, etc. Include those who do not get paid for their work, whether it is parenting, community work, or volunteering.

Remember that you can vary those doing the interview also, or even make it a conversation between two vocations. Panels can also be effective, especially if panellists have questions beforehand. The interviews work most effectively if interviewees have had time to think about the questions but are not reading off notes.

Linking in Interviews

It may be appropriate to link the interview with different components of the service or with the calendar. The church could interview a teacher at the beginning of the school year, a maternity nurse in spring, and accountants at the end of the financial year. Or the interview may link in with the theme of the sermon, with a new song being introduced, with an event coming up, or with a new strategic push for the church.

Commissioning

After interviewing, it may be effective to ask everyone in the same vocational grouping to stand for prayer. For example, call all health workers for a nurse, those in business for an accountant, all who work in trades for an electrician, and those in hospitality for a chef.

Lynn in Singapore told me about the power of being commissioned. She was working in insurance, and her company had invited her to take up a posting in Beijing, China. Her church contacted her and asked if she would come to the evening service to be commissioned for her new opportunity.

At first, she thought it a mistake. "I'm not a missionary," she explained. "You are the best sort of missionary," the pastor responded, "We don't have to pay for you!" As a result of being commissioned and sent by her church to her new role, Lynn saw her work in Beijing through fresh eyes. She focused on relationships and realised that people were hungry to talk about Christianity.

The commissioning may be relatively informal, or you may choose to have a more formal commissioning service. The following liturgy is a well-used example:[4].

Leader:

The Lord appeared to Moses in a burning bush and called to him saying, "Put off your shoes from your feet, for the place on which you are standing is holy ground." Now, by virtue of the indwelling presence of the Holy Spirit, every place we tread becomes holy.

Today, we come to affirm that the work you do each day takes place on holy ground, and as your spiritual leaders, to offer our support and prayers for you and the work to which God has called you.

(Those who wish to be commissioned move forward or stand.)

---

[4] This liturgy has been adapted from several sources including the graduate ministry of Intervarsity Christian Fellowship at Harvard, and Church of the Savior in Washington, DC.

Leader:

From the beginning of creation, we see God at work, laboring over His creation. Jesus himself dignified the workplace by spending the larger part of his earthly life working as a carpenter. Paul affirmed work when he commanded it to be done "with all your heart, as working for the Lord". He saw doing your work as an act of worship, as much as singing a hymn.

> *(The leader asks these commissioning questions, and the commissioned respond, "I do".)*

Leader:

- Brothers and sisters, are you, so far as you know your own heart, called by God to serve him in the workplace?
- Do you trust in Jesus Christ as your Saviour, acknowledging him as Lord of your daily work?
- Do you accept the authority of Scripture, and commit to do your daily work according to God's commands, as the Holy Spirit enables you to?
- Do you affirm that every ability, resource, opportunity, and success come from God's hand, to be used for his glory?
- Will you seek to serve as a faithful servant in your daily work, putting the interests of others above your own?
- Do you accept the responsibility as God's ambassador to your workplace, and hold yourself accountable to God and the body of Christ for your witness?

People to be commissioned:

Enabled by God's indwelling strength, I will endeavour to make each day's work an act of worship. I pray that servanthood, grace, and humility will replace any greed, selfishness, and pride that would taint my work and make it an unworthy offering to you. Amen

The congregation:
As the Body of Christ, we pledge our support, encouragement, and affirmation to these brothers and sisters in Christ, in their successes and in their failures. We recognise them as Christ's ambassadors, in the name of the Father, and of the Son, and of the Holy Spirit. Amen. [5]

---

[5] Adapted from a resource at the Center for Faith & Work, LeTourneau University: "Workplace Commissioning Liturgy" http://centerforfaithandwork.com/sites/default/files/PDFs/Everything_Commissioning_Service_2012.pdf (cited 18-Dec-2017).

Prayer:

Dearest Lord,

You have given us the ability to communicate and to connect via stories.

Thank you for the opportunity to give and receive.

Help us to learn from each other.

Help us to encourage one another to be your holy people at work:

To worship you with our work, and to make a difference for your kingdom.

AMEN

Taking It Further:

1

If you do not do interviews with workers, consider what needs to be done to make it happen. If you already do interviews, are there some other questions here that you could try?

2

Watch the TTT YouTube clip. What do you learn from the interviewee? What do you learn from the interviewer? How well was the interview set up? How could it be used most effectively in a church service?

3

Review the Bible verses used in Mullins' All of Life questions. How appropriate are the verses? Are there any others you could refer to?

4

Consider adapting the Commissioning Service for your church and tradition, and running it. You could choose a vocational grouping, or simply start with a congregation member who is commencing a new job.

Chapter 16

Visiting the Workplace

I was teaching a unit on workplace ministry at a theological college, and I asked the class of 24 how many had been visited in their workplace, by their pastor. Two hands went up.

The first student was a barista in a café, and his pastor had had coffee with him, then asked how the church could have access to discounted catering. The second student revealed that his pastor was fascinated by the tour he gave him of the factory where he worked, and then proceeded to use the things he had seen as sermon illustrations for the next few months.

Neither pastor had spoken to the students about the work they were doing, the challenges they faced, or the gospel needs in the workplace. Both pastors were more focused on what the church could extract from the workplace.

Yet, neither student would ever forget that their pastor had visited them at work.

Gap Between Willingness and Practice

A survey by LeTourneau University in the US found that 98% of pastors expressed a desire to visit the workplaces of church members. However, the survey also found a big gap between willingness and practice:[1]

- 22% of pastors indicate that they make workplace visits once a week.
- 38% visited once or twice a month.
- 21% have made visits less than once a month.

---

[1] "Pastors Want to Visit Church Members' Workplaces Survey Shows", *Center for Faith & Work*. http://centerforfaithandwork.com/article/pastors-want-visit-church-members%E2%80%99-work-places-survey-shows (cited 18-Dec-2017). An update on this survey reveals even more interesting data. Even though there is a trend toward increasing faith and work focus in US churches, people in the congregations still do not value their work as highly as 'professional Christian roles'. A longitudinal study has found that 70% of Christian church attenders still cannot envision how the work they do serves God, and 78% feel their work is less important than the work of a pastor or priest (http://www.centerforfaithandwork.com/article/gap-between-pulpit-pew-narrowing-read-latest-research, cited 18-Dec-2017).

I suspect the figures outside America would be even lower. Further, the survey did not make any assessment of the quality of the visits, on whether they were focused on the church member or church business.

An earlier survey by the same university revealed that 67% of pastors question their understanding of workplace issues.

The Benefits of Visitation
Visiting church members in their places of work has multiple benefits:

- It increases the confidence of pastors in addressing the issues of faith and work integration.
- It is incredibly affirming for church members, helping to validate where they spend 60% of their waking lives.
- It provides opportunities for pastors to gather sermon illustrations, pick up observations and application for sermon application, and look for opportunities for gospel renewal of the workplace.
- There are follow-up prospects such as an interview in church, opportunity to network with others, or even simply more targeted chatting after church.
- It helps pastors see what the training needs are for workers in their congregations.

Examples of Transformed Relationships
After sharing this idea with one particular group, a participant said he realised that when he visited members of his congregation, he often went with an agenda of church business rather than of seeking to learn about them and their work and concerns.

He gave the example of meeting a small business owner at a local café, and the church member receiving an urgent call from work. This pastor gave him permission to take the call and respond. The church member explained he needed to return to work immediately. The pastor asked if he could go with him.

That simple act has transformed his relationship with that church member, and others he has since visited. That pastor is able to speak more clearly into their working lives, and they in return are more open to listen.

Alistair Mackenzie gives this example of the power of pastors visiting workplaces:

"British Baptist Pastor David Coffey says, 'In my time as a Pastor I made a regular pattern to visit church members in their place of work, whenever this was appropriate. I sat with the defence lawyer in a court room; I have watched a farmer assist in the birth of a calf; I have spent time with a cancer consultant in his hospital; I have walked the floor of a chemical factory and sat in the office of a manager who runs a large bookshop. I have driven a tank and spent time with some senior military officers; I have shared the tears and joys of family life with homemakers; I have visited a London hostel for the homeless and walked round a regional prison with a Governor. The purpose of such visits is primarily to encourage and disciple a church member in that place where God has called them to be a worker."[2]

Do What Jesus Did

Greg Forster provides biblical inspiration for visiting the workplace — the fact that Jesus visited workplaces. Forster quotes R. Paul Stevens in his book *Work Matters,* that 122 out of Jesus' 132 public appearances were in the marketplace. Jesus spent the majority of his life humbly working in an ordinary job. He demonstrated his awareness of the workplace through his parables, with 45 of 52 parables set in the marketplace: "fields, sheepfolds, vineyards, kitchens, palaces, courts, fisheries, and more."[3]

---

[2] See: "The Equipping Church Overview", *Theology of Work Project.* https://www.theologyofwork. org/key-topics/the-equipping-church (cited 18-Dec-2017).

[3] Greg Forster, "Pastor, Why Not Visit Their Workplace?" *The Gospel Coalition,* 27 October 2017. https://www.thegospelcoalition.org/article/pastor-why-not-visit-their-workplace (cited 18-Dec-2017).

Ideas for Enabling Visitation

Take Your Church to Work

While I was working at Ridley College's Marketplace Institute, I pioneered a program called Take Your Church to Work. Put simply, it was an opportunity for church staff to gain an immersive experience of work, beyond the lunchtime visitation, and then to debrief and gain ideas for application.

It consisted of:

- Workplace experience: each staff member shadows a congregation member for half a day in their workplace.
- Lunchtime debrief: staff come together to share their experiences.
- Facilitated workshop: a faith–work specialist assists the staff team to draw lessons from the experiences for use in sermons, small group ministry, and even outreach in local communities.
- Dinner sharing: staff and congregation members come together to share their learning.

Where churches had a small number on staff, they could network with other local churches to run the program.

Take Your Pastor to Lunch

Church members do not need to wait for their pastor to initiate. Tom Nelson started a Take Your Pastor to Lunch initiative which included this sample invitation:

Dear [pastor name],

I hope this note finds you well. I have something important I would like to discuss with you.

I've been thinking about how my faith intersects with my work lately and would love your counsel. When your schedule permits, I would like to buy you lunch and discuss how to better minister in the area of influence in which God has placed me here at work. Rather than meet at a restaurant, I'd like you to come by my place of work first, so you can have an idea about what I do between Sundays. I also think it would be great for you to meet some of my co-workers so that perhaps some of their misconceptions about pastors can be corrected. It might even open an opportunity to invite them to our church.

Most importantly, I highly respect your leadership and ministry in my life and would be delighted to spend more time getting to know you on a personal level. Please let me know what dates would work best for you.

[Sign your normal close][your name][4]

Conversation Starters

Nelson also includes some conversation starters for the Take Your Pastor to Lunch initiative:

Suggestions to begin:

- 🌙 Tell your pastor how much you appreciate the ministry of the church.
- 🌙 Comment on a recent sermon that touched you in some way.
- 🌙 Show your pastor around and introduce co-workers as it's appropriate and doesn't disturb their work.
- 🌙 As you visit, explain what you do on a daily basis.
- 🌙 Mention any specific struggles that people in your line of work deal with.

Questions to foster discussion:

- 🌙 How can I best use my workplace skills to serve the church?
- 🌙 Does the church see a distinction between church work and my work?
- 🌙 How does the church see 'secular' work fitting in God's kingdom?
- 🌙 How does my work fit or not fit in God's kingdom?

---

[4] "Sample Invitation: Take Your Pastor to Lunch", *Celebrate Your Work*. http://celebrateyourwork. com/take-your-pastor-to-lunch/sample-invitation-to-take-your-pastor-to-lunch/#.V47yU1czFSU (cited 18-Dec-2017).

- How can you and/or the church help me connect my work and faith?
- Would you be willing to help me find answers to these questions from the Bible?

Close your time with prayer:
- How can I pray for you?
- May I share some confidential requests for you personally to pray for me?[5]

---

[5] "Conversation Starters: Take Your Pastor to Lunch", *Celebrate Your Work*. http://celebrateyourwork. com/take-your-pastor-to-lunch/conversation-starters-take-your-pastor-to-lunch/#.WjkW-WLSZ1-U (cited 18-Dec-2017).

Prayer:

Loving God,

You created this world, worked with us, and walked with us.

You visited us with angelic messengers.

You visited in visions and dreams.

You visited us on earth in the shape of Jesus.

Jesus visited so many places of work.

Help us as workers to invite our pastor to our work.

Help us as workers to support other workers.

Help us as pastors to visit workplaces and support workers.

Grant us new insights into our workplaces as we share what we see.

Build our knowledge of how our work can be impacted by the gospel.

AMEN

Taking It Further:

1

If you do visit people in their workplaces, note what you find helpful about the experience. What tips from this chapter will you use?

2

Review the questions Tom Nelson has written for Take Your Pastor to Lunch. Write down answers to the questions. Which will you need to do more research on? What other questions would you add? Are there training programs that could flow from the questions?

3

Read through the Gospel of Matthew and note the following:
- Where did Jesus spend his time in Matthew's Gospel? (Clue: Chapters 2–4, 8–9, 11, 13–17, 21, 26)
  - What did he teach? (Focus on chapters 5–7)
- What illustrations did Jesus use? (Find aspirational images, animals, working situations, his own working context, Old Testament heroes)

4

If you are a pastor, analyse the possibility of running Take Your Church to Work with your team, or linking with other local churches. What are the issues? What would be the advantages? Plan out the resources. If you are a workplace Christian, analyse the possibility of Take Your Pastor to Lunch. Draft the email. What are the issues? What would be the advantages?

Chapter 17

Training Workplace Christians

For the last 24 years, the focus of my working has been in training and education. This has been wonderful because I **love** teaching and learning! One of the greatest pleasures of life for me is when a participant in a lecture, seminar, or training course has that 'Aha' moment. They suddenly 'get it' and begin to see the world differently.

As a mother, the most intense training periods of my life have been teaching my children how to drive. It was always a battle between confidence and competence. When they started they lacked confidence and competence, and frankly, it was terrifying! However, as we progressed there were times when they were more confident than they should have been regarding their skills, and I would have to warn them to be more cautious. Just before the driving exam, their competence was greater than their confidence, and I would encourage them that their skills were sufficient.

In church situations, we train for confidence and competence in those areas we consider important for Christian discipleship. We teach people how to lead Bible studies, how to be involved in the music program, how to pray, and how to run various parts of the service. We have programs on pastoral care training and evangelism. We encourage people to go to conferences to deepen their understanding of the Bible, or to engage in missional activity.

All this training prepares people for what happens *within* the church. Rarely do we train people how to apply their faith where they spend 95% of their time, outside the church.

What Do Workplace Christians Want to Know?
Tom Nelson, in writing for the Center for Faith & Work at LeTourneau University, has written a series of questions that working congregation members would like to explore with their pastors:

- Is the work I do outside church important to God?
- What's the biblical purpose of business?
- What does a robust Monday-morning faith look like?
- What are the ethical dimensions for a Christian in business?

- What kind of corporate culture should I help create as a follower of Christ?
- How should I treat employees as a Christian boss?
- What products and services can, should, and shouldn't be offered?
- How should I talk about my faith in the workplace?
- How can a business contribute to human flourishing and God's kingdom?[1]

These questions are a great starting place for thinking about the sort of training program churches could run to prepare Christians to express their faith in the workplace.

What Should Training Look Like?

There are many different methods and opportunities for training. Here are a few ideas that have worked in churches.

A series of seminars

A large church wanted to prepare their evening congregation, made up mostly of young workers, for the workforce. I ran a series of seminars under the title Faith@Work. For each seminar, I interviewed a worker from the congregation to illustrate the good of work, how working is cursed, and how work can be redeemed. It was wonderful for the congregation to hear these stories.

Seminar 1: Work is *good*

- Dealt briefly with the sacred-secular split, on why we struggle to connect our Sunday church experience with our Monday work experience.
- Introduced the concept of work as our mission field, for which we need to be prepared.

---

[1] "Pastors Want to Visit Church Members' Workplaces Survey Shows", *Center for Faith & Work*. http://centerforfaithandwork.com/article/pastors-want-visit-church-members%E2%80%99-work-places-survey-shows (cited 26-Feb-2018).

- Used Bible verses to examine the concept that work is good — that we are made in the image of a working God, who invites us to join him in his creative and sustaining work.
- Challenged to think about ways we can apply that knowledge in our workplaces.
- Gave us an opportunity to learn from someone about the good of their work.

Seminar 2: Working is *cursed*

- Used Bible verses to examine the concept that work is cursed — that as a result of the fall our working will be frustrating and less fruitful, and that work relationships will be difficult.
- Challenged us to think about ways we can apply that knowledge in our workplaces.
- Gave us an opportunity to learn from someone about very negative or frustrating work situations.
- Talked about the particular struggles Christians face in the workplace.
- Finished with the need to balance the good and the bad of working.

Seminar 3: Work can be *redeemed*

- Used Bible verses to examine the concept that work can be redeemed — that Jesus' mission was to redeem every part of our lives, and we have spiritual gifts to apply in every situation.
- Allowed us to break into vocation groups to discuss ideas of how we might attempt to redeem our workplaces.
- Gave us an opportunity to hear an inspiring story from someone who has experienced redemption in the work context.
- Explored different practical ways of glorifying God in the workplace.
- Finished with a commissioning service, where we prayed, read, and made commitments about serving God in our working.

Small/Focus/Community/Connect/Bible study groups
I have heard from churches who have used excellent resources available for teaching through small groups. These include the following:

-) *ReFrame*, prepared by the Marketplace Institute at Regent College. It is a high-quality series of ten sessions that covers the full story of the Bible and challenges us to apply the learning in every area of our lives, including our working. Utilising the faculty of Regent College, as well as guest interviews, it is biblically true, relevant, and engaging. It needs a minimum of two hours per session.[2]
-) *Fruitfulness on the Frontline*, prepared by the London Institute for Contemporary Christianity.[3] Besides the book by Mark Greene, there is a DVD with a leader's guide, children's resources, sample sermons, and a 40-day prayer guide. It is an eight–session series that talks about everyone's frontlines, which is where they spend most of their time: workplace, neighbourhood, home, community. There is a follow-up resource, *Whole Life Worship* by Sam & Sara Hargreaves, which is also excellent and helps churches respond to the challenge of fostering whole-life discipleship.[4]
-) *Gospel Shaped Work*, from the Gospel Coalition and featuring Tom Nelson. This comprehensive whole-church resource features a DVD with eight sessions, personal Bible study devotions, group Bible studies and a personal journal. It is part of the Gospel Shaped series which includes worship, outreach, living, and mercy.[5]
-) *Gospel-Centred Work: Becoming the Worker God Wants You to Be,* from Tim Chester. This is part of a series on Gospel-centred church, life, marriage, family, and leadership:[6]
  - (Part 1: Gospel work (God works, Nothing works, Jesus works, Good work)

---

[2] http://www.reframecourse.com/ (cited 18-Dec-2017).
[3] http://www.licca.org.uk/splash/index.html (cited 18-Dec-2017).
[4] Available from the LICC website and bookshops, published by InterVarsity Press, 2017.
[5] http://gsc.thegospelcoalition.org/work/ (cited 18-Dec-2017).
[6] Tim Chester, *Gospel-Centred Work* (Surrey: The Good Book Company, 2013).

- Part 2: Transforming work (I'm worried about my work, I'm afraid of my boss, I can't bear to fail, I find it hard to stop, I can't get on with them)
- Part 3: Mission work (Blessing, Decisions, Witness, Community)
- Conclusion (God at work)

- *In God's Service: Being Distinctive in Your Workplace*, by Andrew Laird and Steven Naoum. This series aims to encourage Christians at work to be 'salt of the earth and light of the world'. Laird and Naoum have applied this biblical truth to being a distinctive disciple at work through a variety of workplace challenges. There are ten studies aimed at Bible study groups, along with ten Bible 'bites' that take about 10 to 15 minutes, best done during the commute to work or lunch break.[7]

- *Alpha in the Workplace*: There is a specific Alpha course designed for workplace settings. It is a practical introduction to the Christian faith for the workplace environment and is open to anyone. It runs as a series of weekly meetings with a meal, a talk and small group discussion. There are 15 talks over a 10-week period that cover the basic principles of the Christian faith. The regular sessions can be held at lunchtime or after work.[8]

Whole church focus

One church in Melbourne, Australia, ran an integrated program with a focus on mission in the workplace. There was a teaching program covering the theology of work. There were two seminars on workplace evangelism and apologetics in the workplace. There were coordinated small group studies for deeper discussions and learning. This was followed by a week of missional activity where workers were encouraged to live out their faith in the workplace. It concluded with a celebration service where people shared their stories.

---

[7] Andrew Laird and Steven Naoum, *In God's Service: Being Distinctive in Your Workplace* (Sydney Missionary and Bible College, 2015).

[8] For Singapore, see: http://singapore.alpha.org/workplace/ (cited 28-Dec-2017).

Topics for Training

Like most training, it is best to start with a needs assessment. A simple survey can ascertain areas of interest, skill areas where people lack confidence, and the biblical foundation required to support the activity.

While it would be impossible to develop a complete list, the chapter headings of *Workship* (Volumes 1 and 2) could help as a list for people to engage with. Following is a 10-week outline for exploring workplace Christians:

A biblical foundation
- A biblical understanding of work
- Apologetics for the workplace

Spiritual disciplines for working
- Sharing my faith at work
- Praying at work and for work

On God's mission at work
- Discovering my vocation
- Jesus-shaped leadership
- Redeeming work
- Work and cultural renewal

Being salt and light at work
- Tackling ethical issues
- Work–life balance.

Integrated Training

As with most training, it is only effective if training is modelled and refreshed regularly, and if it becomes part of the culture of the church — "The way we do things around here". This means that it should be backed up with sermons, church services, interviews, and workplace visits that reinforce the learning. You will notice that Jesus exemplified this consistency. His teaching was lived out in conversations and actions, demonstrating what whole-life discipleship to God looks like.

Wesley Methodist Church Singapore is a large church (about 7,000 members) that has a four-year plan[9] culminating with a goal to impact society. The church leadership recognised that this involved the church changing its focus from an inward-looking attractional model, to an outward-looking missional model.

The church has been strategic in moving towards this goal. To start workplace Christians thinking about their jobs differently, it has committed to holding an annual marketplace conference. The first one focused on the theology of work, the second one focused on being witnesses for Christ in the different vocations, and the third one will be supporting fellow believers in living out their faith in the workplace. The numbers have grown from 400 in the first year to a third year target of 1,000. To keep the momentum going between each annual conference, three marketplace seminars are run. These attract smaller numbers but are more practical, addressing things such as business ethics, challenges in working in a foreign country, job transitions, and so on.

The church has also commenced forming marketplace support groups (MSG), each consisting of several junior workers and one more experienced worker in a specific vocation. It was piloted with a group of lawyers, and now there are seven vocational-based groups running. In addition, every MSG facilitator in the church was given a copy of the first volume of *Workship*. They have also utilised a mentoring resource by Soo-Inn Tan, *3–2–1: Following Jesus in Threes*[10].

This is Wesley's marketplace ministry's vision:

- *We want to see church members, most of whom are in the marketplace, having a sense of calling to their jobs.*
- *We want them to see themselves as salt and light in the workplace.*
- *We want them to recognise that they are ministers where they are in their ordinary work.*

---

[9] Direction 2020 (2017-2020) intentionally focuses on three broad themes to live out the church's mission: Growing in Christ, Building Community, and Impacting the World (2019 – 2020).

[10] See: https://graceworks.com.sg/store/category/christian-living/3-2-1-following-jesus-in-threes/ (cited 28-Dec-2017).

- *We want them to see their daily work as God's work, and as a Christian witness.*
- *We want them to cultivate Christian character and demonstrate Christian values.*
- *We want them to see the importance of relationships at work, that there is a consistency in seeing and working with people, and that every day they may be able to move a person slightly closer to Christ by the irresistibility of their words or behaviour.[11]*

---

[11] From an interview with Patrick Chua, Pastoral Team Member, Witness & Evangelism Ministry, Wesley Methodist Church in December, 2017.

Prayer:

Gracious God,

You have given us your Word as a precious resource to teach us about you and your world.

You have given us your Son Jesus as the perfect example of your teaching lived out.

You have given us your Spirit to empower and encourage us to live as your disciples in every place we do our work, whether paid or unpaid.

You have given us your Church to enable and support us to be the best people we can be, made in your image and redeemed by your Son, and given the ministry of reconciling all people and the whole world to you.

Help us to take every opportunity to build our knowledge and skills, so we can work most effectively to honour you,

AMEN

Taking It Further:

1

Jot down some responses to the questions listed from Tom Nelson. Where do you need to do more research? Discuss them in your small group or with your pastor.

2

Check out the resources listed for small groups. See if you can pilot one of the resources for the church, with the intention of encouraging other groups to follow. Explore the possibility of doing the studies in vocational groupings.

3

Read Luke 9:1–9, and 10:1–24. Look at the example of Jesus' training as he sent out his disciples. What do you notice about his methodology? How did he prepare people? What skills, knowledge, and attitudes did he want to impart? How did he follow up on the training?

4

Outline a faith and work training strategy for your church. If you are the pastor of your church, form a small planning group representing the diversity of people and working roles. If you are not the pastor, begin with a meeting with your pastor. Design a needs analysis. Work out the topics that need to be covered and the best methods of imparting those skills, knowledge inputs, and attitudes. Ensure that you incorporate examples of working in the training, maximising input from the congregation. Analyse resources available to assist in the delivery and follow-up. Schedule what needs to happen to make the strategy a reality.

Chapter 18

Mentoring Workers

Christine was a passionate Christian, having combined Bible college with her university studies, and even spending time in a Christian community. She was intricately involved in her church. She led services, discipled young Christians, facilitated a Bible study, played in the worship band, and prayed during church services.

When she came to me for mentoring, she was considering two offers to plant churches. The first was an experimental service connected with her current church, specifically aimed at young workers. The second was a community church based in her share house. She was well-equipped for both opportunities.

However, within six months she had dropped out of church and wandered a long way from the faith she had grown up with. This came through a process of gentle questioning which revealed a huge gap between her mind and her heart. She had gone through some suffering, and failed to sufficiently process her emotions.

As we reflected on her experiences and emotions, we also began to untangle her thinking. There was another gap we uncovered — one between what she thought she should believe, and all the questions that had begun to accumulate, particularly during her university studies.

Much of our discussions revolved around the issues that were being thrown up by her studies and her working: questions of identity, exploration of vocation, and apologetic questions around whether Jesus was an historical figure and whether he claimed to be Christ.

While she is currently not attending church, she has often said that I am one of the forces attracting her toward God, while there are many forces pulling her away.

Perhaps you think I should have given an example of a more successful Christian mentoring. However, I think this story and its challenges illustrate how mentoring is one of the most significant services that churches can provide for their congregations.

The Crisis of Church Attendance

Many churches are finding it harder to get people to attend services regularly. The hole in most congregations is in the 20 to 39-year-old age range. The US figures are extraordinary: the Barna Group report that 60% of young adults who grew up in the church drop out, and 30% say that church is not at all important, while a further 40% are largely ambivalent.[1]

Australia's congregations are also losing young adults. According to the research as charted below, those in their 20s and 30s represent 20% of the *church* population but 29% of the *general* Australian population in 2011. In a 2014 update, McCrindle research reported the gap had widened further with 20–39-year-olds now 34% of the population, but just 21% of church-goers.[2]

The age profile of Australian church attenders across 23 Catholic, Anglican and Protestant denominations.

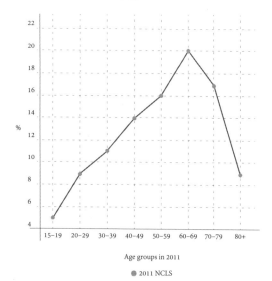

Age groups in 2011

● 2011 NCLS

Source: 2011 NCLS Attender Survey (n = 227,063)[3]

---

[1] "What Millennials Want When They Visit Church", *Barna*, 4 March 2015. https://www.barna.org/barna-update/millennials/711-what-millennials-want-when-they-visit-church#.V5wh9pN95-U (cited 26-Feb-2018).

[2] "A demographic snapshot of Christianity and church attenders in Australia", McCrindle, 18 April 2014. http://www.mccrindle.com.au/resources/A-Demographic-snapshot-of-Christianity-and-church-attenders-in-Australia_McCrindle.pdf (cited 26-Feb-2018).

[3] Reference: Powell, R., Brady, M., Jacka, K., Pepper, M., & Sterland, S. (2011). *2011 Australia Church Life Profile*. Sydney: NCLS Research (cited 28-Dec-2017).

Why Millennials Do and Don't Attend Church

Barna Group has done extensive research of why that age group does not attend church. While this research is based in the US, there are similar reports from Asia, and all the explanations ring true for the millennials I have worked amongst in Australia. For those who do not attend, the top reasons are:

- I find God elsewhere
- It's not relevant to me
- Church is boring

While those who have remained in the church say it is important because:

- I go to be closer to God
- I learn about God there
- The Bible says to go[4]

Connecting with Millennials

In their follow-up research, the Barna Group identified five ways to connect with millennials:

1. *Make room for meaningful relationships.* Close personal friendships with adults are a significant factor in millennials staying (59%). Of those staying, half of them reported a mentoring relationship.
2. *Teach cultural discernment.* Millennials need guidance in meaningfully engaging with culture and applying their faith to the problems they encounter in the world.
3. *Create reverse mentoring opportunities.* Millennials want to be helped to discover their purpose and mission in the world,

---

[4] "What Millennials Want When They Visit Church", *Barna*, 4 March 2015. https://www.barna.org/barna-update/millennials/711-what-millennials-want-when-they-visit-church#.V5wh9pN95-U (cited 26-Feb-2018).

with opportunities to serve the poor, expand their thinking, and find a cause that motivates them.

4. *Teach the connection between vocation and discipleship.* Millennials want help in discerning their calling and how they can apply their unique gifts and skills in the world, whether in the church or beyond.

5. *Facilitate connection with Jesus.* Millennials want to experience the Bible as authoritative, and providing wisdom for a meaningful life. They also want to experience an intimate relationship with Jesus.[5]

The Importance of Mentoring

Mentoring is significant for helping all age groups to remain connected with faith and church, but it is especially pivotal for millennials. Mentoring enables the deep relationships that young people crave. It is an opportunity for them to be taught and have modelled the way faith can be applied to the problems they see. Mentoring can lead to opportunities to express their gifts. It is a means of helping them discern their giftings and find their callings. It also assists them to experience firsthand the good use of the Bible as the authoritative word of God, and as application in everyday life.

Modes of Mentoring

Australian mentoring expert John Mallison identified the many facets of mentoring that can be applied.[6]

---

[5] "5 Ways to Connect with Millennials", *Barna*, 9 September 2014. https://www.barna.com/research/5-ways-to-connect-with-millennials/ (cited 26-Feb-2018).
[6] See John Mallison, *Mentoring to develop disciples & leaders*, full text available online here: http://www.johnmallison.com/jmmentorbook/.

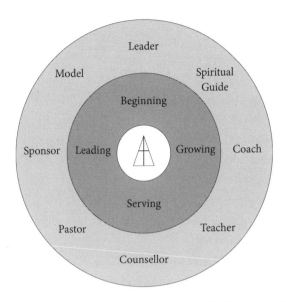

The inner circle represents the Trinity, with the recognition that Jesus, symbolised by the cross, is at the centre of what we do as mentors.

The dark circle represents the stages the mentoree goes through in the mentoring relationships. There will be a beginning of the relationship, or beginning of faith. Often there is a rapid period of growth in the mentoree at the start. Progressing on, a mentor should encourage the mentoree to acts of service of God and others. The goal for many mentoring relationships is to grow the mentoree to a position of leadership.

The outside circle represents all the different roles that a mentor might have within the relationship, and these correlate with the different stages.

- At the beginning the mentor is quite clearly the leader, the source of information and modelling behaviour.
- As the mentoree grows, the mentor uses the roles of spiritual guide, coach, and teacher.
- When the mentoree has the experience of serving, the mentor may counsel for issues that come up or provide pastoral support.

❯ As the mentoree develops into a leader, the mentor acts as a sponsor, creating opportunities, and models good leadership behaviour.

Jesus Mentoring His Disciples

We can see these different modes of mentoring in the way Jesus interacted with his disciples. He also demonstrated some of the following characteristics:

❯ *Available*: Jesus was more physically available to his disciples than we may have the opportunity to be. However, with technology, we can be just as accessible.

❯ *Personal*: Jesus seemed to have customised some of his lessons for the roles or issues the disciples had. There is no canned method of mentoring.

❯ *Dialogue*: Jesus mostly communicated through conversation, particularly in asking questions. Rather than the expert–novice model of mentoring, Jesus challenged his disciples to think through issues.

❯ *Listened*: Jesus then listened carefully to responses. He affirmed what was good and corrected what was wrong.

❯ *Applied biblical wisdom*: Jesus often quoted Scripture in his encounters with others.

❯ *Identified obstacles*: Jesus helped the disciples see problems and work out solutions, both for themselves and for others.

❯ *Prayed*: Jesus prayed often. We also see in John 17:6–19 a beautiful model of prayer for mentorees.

❯ *Cared for his own soul*: Alongside his time with others, Jesus went away on his own to spend time with God and to pray.[7]

---

[7] These characteristics have been developed from a list compiled by Bruce Demarest and quoted by Rick Lewis, in *Mentoring Matters* (Grand Rapids: Monarch Books, 2009), 117.

Fresh Expressions of Mentoring

Most of my experience is in the business world, where mentoring is seen as critical for developing leaders and keeping employees engaged. The most highly-respected mentoring guide used in business is by Lois Zachary. She has documented the change in modern mentoring from a traditional mentor/apprentice model to the following:

- Mentoree role: from passive receiver to active partner.
- Mentor role: From authority to facilitator.
- Learning process: from mentor-directed to mentoree self-directed.
- Length of relationship: from calendar focused to goal determined.
- Mentoring relationship: from one mentor to multiple mentors, as well as group and peer mentoring models.
- Setting: from face-to-face to multiple and varied venues.
- Focus: from content-oriented (knowledge and information) to process-oriented (critical reflection and application).[8]

Different Types of Mentoring

Mentorees may seek different types of mentoring depending on their needs. You may even move among these different kinds with the same mentoree.

- *Structured Bible studies*: to demonstrate the authority of the Bible, increase knowledge, and show application of the Bible, particularly to working situations.
- *Dealing with a particular issue*: you may focus on a particular issue for a period of time, whether it be a question of faith, seeking a calling, or dealing with ethical issues at work. The mentoring may end after that learning experience, or continue on.
- *Skills development*: this is more commonly termed coaching. It may be skills of Jesus-shaped leadership, disciple-making, or apologetics.

---

[8] Lois Zachary, *The Mentor's Guide: Facilitating Effective Learning Relationships* (San Francisco: Jossey-Bass, 2012), 6.

- *Exploring spiritual practices*: there is an increasing interest in spiritual disciplines, which may not be well-known in some modern church traditions. The role of mentor here might be as a spiritual director. A good place to start with workers is the six spiritual disciplines described in Volume 1 of *Workship*. For more details, see Appendix 2.
- *Open-ended*: it may be a casual mentoring relationship, or an intentional friendship, with the goal of 'doing life' with one another.
- *Accountability*: there may be a a particular temptation at work, or an area of sin that needs to be dealt with; or the mentoree may want to be held accountable for developing a spiritual practice such as regular Bible reading or praying for the workplace.
- *Prayer focus*: some mentoring relationships are based around a regular sharing then praying for needs and concerns.
- *All of life*: this is perhaps the classic mentoring style of John Stott, Jonathan Edwards, and so on. Like Jesus, this involves the mentoree moving in with the mentor and learning from close observation. This provides the opportunity for 'teachable moments' that come up at unexpected times.

Note: In Appendix 2 there is an outline of mentoring sessions to run through with the spiritual disciplines described in Section 2 of Volume 1 of *Workship*.

Methods of Mentoring Workers
While it is better if mentoring relationships develop naturally, some structure and training can ensure that no one misses out.

Structure. The simplest way is to link a more experienced Christian and a younger worker within the same vocational group. This allows them to identify the common issues within a vocation, and means that context does not need to be explained in as much detail. Alternative forms are peer or group mentoring. Advertising opportunities and having a list for mentors and mentorees allows maximum participation. However, there should be a vetting of volunteers and provision of training.

Training. The basic form of training involves specific practice of the critical skills of mentoring:

Listening
Asking questions
Discerning emotions
Building relationships
Focusing on the spiritual growth of the other.

One of the most effective training methods I have used is getting an experienced mentor in a room and asking him or her to conduct a mentoring session with a mentoree while the class watched (obviously, provide boundaries on the level of sharing). Half the class made notes on content, the other half made notes on process such as body language, the way questions were asked, setting, and so on. The learning was very insightful, and students could ask the mentor why he or she did certain things in a particular way.

The Dos and Don'ts of Mentoring
The mentoring experience can be enhanced by following some simple rules:

Do	Don't
Ask good questions	Judge
Be mutually accountable	Blame
Show mutual respect	Interpret from own frame of
Focus on areas where Christians can stray	reference
	Try to fix/rescue
Be real: laugh, cry, have fun	Jump to conclusions
Occasionally do something different: a meal, movie, retreat, lecture, etc.	Watch the clock/check phone…
	Finish sentences
	Interrupt

Prayer:

Our Rabbi and Teacher,

Thank you for providing the example of Jesus in mentoring.

Help us to be wise as we seek to mentor others.

Help us to be conscious that we are always being watched, and we are always modelling behaviour and attitudes to others.

Help us to be intentional and strategic in our approaches to mentoring.

Lead us to the people you want us to mentor, and lead them to us.

Guide us so we can teach others to be more effective in serving you and others at work.

AMEN

Taking It Further:

1

Analyse your own church demographics. What age group is missing? How can you attract them? What work issues may be relevant to them?

2

Analyse a key mentoring relation you have experienced. Which of the different modes of mentoring did your mentor use? How many of the mentoree stages did you go through? What have you learnt through the analysis?

3

Read through the four gospel accounts and note down examples of the ways Jesus mentored his disciples, according to the checklist provided. What do you notice about his availability? Whom did he get personal with among the disciples? And so on.

4

Map out a mentoring program for yourself, your Bible study group, or your church. How will you structure the program? What training will you provide? What types of mentoring will you advocate? What resources will you provide? How will you publicise the program? How will you monitor the program and evaluate its success? Pray carefully through each step of the process.

Chapter 19
Chaplaincy in the Workplace

I was conducting research for an organisation supporting Christians working in the mining industry. We had received a grant to examine the need for chaplains in the industry.

I called Wayne, a mine manager at a large coalmine in Australia's Hunter Valley. He was a bit curt as I explained the reason for my phone call. When I asked if he thought a chaplain would be useful from the perspective of mining operations, he interrupted me.

"A chaplain? One of those God guys?" he demanded.

"Yes," I replied meekly, wondering where this was going.

"How soon can you get me one?"

"We aren't actually offering them. We're just researching the need."

"I need one in ten minutes," he said.

It turned out that in ten minutes, one of Wayne's best workers was going to walk through the door wanting some advice on marital breakdown.

"I am bloody good at getting huge amounts of dirt out of the ground," explained Wayne, "But I don't know what I'm going to say to this bloke."

"But you have an Employee Assistance Program, and a human resources department," I pointed out.

"That EAP is a psychologist on the end of the phone. What chance do I have of getting this guy to call a perfect stranger and confess that he is failing at his marriage?" said Wayne gruffly. "And who is going to visit his wife and kids? And don't mention human resources to me, they've outsourced this stuff. Get me a chaplain, and get me one quick!"

The Changing Face of Work

As I talked further with Wayne, it dawned on me the extent to which the modern workplace has changed in such a short period of time. My mum stayed at home while we were growing up, was not expected to work, and looked after all domestic concerns, freeing my dad to focus on his work which he did for approximately 60 hours a week.

For me, career was a priority; but I still had the option of caring for my kids, which I did as my primary task, juggling part-time work and my writing business on the side. Once they went to school, I eased back into more regular work.

For most families, one income is not an option. Increasingly both parents are combining work and caring for kids, which is fine unless anyone in the family gets sick. Then options other than childcare are required.

Wayne explained that more and more he is seeing domestic issues entering the sphere of work. His workers are less available and more distracted. There is tremendous pressure on the family unit, which has to run with the precision of a Singaporean Chinese New Year banquet to survive.

Managers like Wayne, trained in technical skills rather than the softer side of leadership who themselves are dedicated to their work, flounder in this environment.

As one workplace chaplaincy provider pointed out, "The workplace is increasingly becoming the primary place of community for many if not most people. For many people, as conflicted as the workplace is, that's where they're spending most of their time, and that's where their primary relationships are."[1]

Organisations respond with EAPs, growing human resource departments, and providing yoga classes at lunchtime, on-site childcare, and flexible work practices.

There is a growing opportunity for chaplains in such an environment. An onsite caring presence demonstrates that the organisation is genuinely invested in its employees, and frees leaders to focus on work outcomes rather than employee wellbeing concerns.

Workplace Chaplaincy

The list of domestic issues impacting the workplace includes addiction, depression, financial difficulty, parenting struggles, domestic violence, elder care, separation or divorce, stress, grief, or suicide.

---

[1] Steve Cook, CEO, quoted in "Workplace chaplains have their believers", *Houston Chronicle*, 12 September 2014. http://www.houstonchronicle.com/business/article/Believers-say-workplace-chaplains-can-be-a-5751092.php (cited 18-Dec-2017).

All these are symptoms of brokenness. The organisation Workplace Chaplains in the United States encourages moving employees from brokenness to wholeness by providing emotional and spiritual support to them.[2]

They seek to reverse the negative cycle of employee brokenness that so easily leads to performance issues, workplace conflict, unfocused work, safety issues, and missed opportunities. They point to the benefits of decreased absenteeism and increased productivity, and freeing up of leadership.

Chaplains have tended to be focused in dangerous industries like defence, mining, emergency services; or places where suffering and/or death occur such as hospitals, aged care centres, and prisons; or places where there are vulnerable people such as schools. Industrial chaplaincy emerged in the 19th Century as a specific outreach of churches to blue collar workers. Today, the growing popularity of corporate chaplaincy is a recognition that wellbeing in the workplace has a spiritual element.

Workplace chaplains provide crisis response, religious services when required (e.g. a funeral service at a remote minesite), visitation to those who are sick or rehabilitating, counseling, conflict resolution, wholeness training, and trusted referral with follow-up.

Formal Chaplaincy

There are various levels of chaplaincy. Formal chaplaincy is a service provided by a specialist organisation. A chaplain is contracted to provide chaplaincy services. It may be a fulltime position, but usually it involves weekly or monthly visits, as well as arrangements for the provision of services for critical incidents.

Peter is contracted through the head office of a mining corporation to provide chaplaincy services to several sites. He is based in a capital city and does a fly-in-fly-out. This arrangement allows him to get involved in the personal lives of miners. He is often called on to run

---

[2] http://www.workplacechaplains.us/ (cited 18-Dec-2017).

baptisms, weddings, or funerals, as he is the only 'God-botherer' people know.

I asked him where he spent most time to get to know those onsite. Without hesitation he said the bar or the crib room. He finds himself advocating for safety, and called upon as a confidante of the general manager, such is the diversity of the role.

Richard provides chaplaincy services to lawyers in a capital city. He counsels them on personal issues, and has a 'ministry of presence' for those struggling with the pressures of the courtroom.

Tony is hired by the council of a town to be a chaplain in the business district. He knows all the shop owners, prays at official occasions, is on hand when there is a break-in or a personal tragedy, and assists the churches to work together.

Although most chaplains are formally trained with a theology degree as well as some form of counseling training, sometimes chaplaincy openings can emerge from circumstance. Jason worked at a mining site and was a keen Christian. When there was a serious accident at the mine, he was on-hand to provide encouragement and support for the workers affected. Mine management offered to create the role of a chaplain for him, which he would fulfill alongside his regular job. He already had great relationships with the workers, and was trusted and respected by management.

Chaplaincy Everywhere

There is an opportunity for every Christian worker to see themselves as an informal chaplain, offering hospitality, care, and counsel within the workplace. The Methodist church in England has capitalised on this idea creating the Chaplaincy Everywhere course.[3] It is a training program aimed at empowering every worker. It has seven sessions and can be taught in small groups covering the following topics:

---

[3] http://www.methodist.org.uk/our-work/our-work-in-britain/chaplaincy/chaplaincy-everywhere/chaplaincy-everywhere-course/ (cited 18-Dec-2017).

- Caught up in the mission of God
- As Christ in the world
- The Spirit of chaplaincy
- The cloak of chaplaincy (Chaplains get their name from the French word for cloak '*capella*', which Martin of Tours offered to a beggar)
- What do chaplains do?
- Chaplains in context
- Job description for a chaplain

Those who complete the course may apply for formal accreditation as a chaplain, or simply be intentional about taking up chaplaincy opportunities in their own workplace.

Prayer:

[*A blessing from the Chaplaincy Everywhere course⁴*]

Go, responding with sensitivity to the nudges of the Holy Spirit.

Go, with eyes open to the needs of those around you.

Go, with the love of God in your heart, knowing that his love is enough.

Enough for you and for the whole world,

Love that is making all things new,

Love that enfolds us in a healing embrace,

Love that is at our end as in our beginning.

Go, with love, in the love of the Father, the Son and the Holy Spirit.

AMEN

---

⁴ http://www.methodist.org.uk/media/3346/chaplaincy-everywhere-session4-0912.pdf (cited 18-Dec-2017).

Taking It Further:

1

Note down any chaplains you have met: at hospital, your children's school, attending your church. What is their role? What qualities make them suited to that role?

2

Check out the links in this chapter: Workplace Chaplains, the article in the *Houston Chronicle,* and the Chaplaincy Everywhere course. What are the key features of chaplaincy? What are some of the reservations as you read? How effective is the Chaplaincy Everywhere course as a resource?

3

Read Romans 12. Write up a job description for an informal chaplain based on this chapter. What is the key goal? What are the main activities for the role? What are the values of a chaplain implied through this passage? What outcomes would flow? What would be the impact of applying this job description in your workplace?

4

Plan to run Chaplaincy Everywhere with your small group, or a vocational grouping in your church. How does the material need to be re-contextualised? How would you structure the training? How would you follow up? What further resources are required?

Chapter 20

Church Presence
in the Workplace

Most people think that the church would not be welcome in the workplace, but there are actually lots of creative ways that churches can make a difference. Most of the time, churches may not realise the impact they are having.

I was visiting a church to talk about faith and work initiatives. The pastor seemed guarded, but then casually commented on something his church had tried without realising it was a brilliant faith and work strategy.

Adopting a Neighbourhood Business

The church had decided to get to know some of the local business owners by inviting them to tell the church the story of their business. They started with a café. The owner Lucy was invited to speak either during or after the church service. She preferred to come after the service.

Most of the congregation stayed behind after that particular service. Lucy turned up and started sharing her passion for coffee and food that had motivated her to open her coffee shop. She spoke of the relationships she had with the customers, and what she loved about being in that area.

When she finished, the pastor told her that for the next month he would ask the congregation to visit Lucy's café, get to know her staff, and bless her business. He then asked if he could pray for her. She reluctantly agreed.

After a month she came back, and this time asked to come *during* the service. She stood up and thanked the congregation, many of whom she knew by name, and told them it had been one of the best months of working she had ever had. She said the presence of church members in the café had made a tangible difference to the atmosphere at the café and her staff had felt personally encouraged.

What was more, she had told other businesses about what the church had done, and they wanted to know when it was their turns!

A Clean-up Campaign in Local Schools

I heard another story from a school principal. Laurie was not a Christian but had been deeply impacted by a church's involvement with his last school. The public school was in a tough area of the city, where the parents had less money and resources were stretched.

The school waited in line for maintenance, but was beginning to look very dilapidated. The pastor of a local church asked to have an appointment with Laurie. The pastor commented on how tired the school looked, and Laurie was waiting for a reprimand. Instead, the pastor asked if he and his church could have a working bee to clean up the school within the next month.

He asked for a list of the jobs that needed to be done, as he planned to arrange access to paint and other resources, and to get some tradespeople organised for simple repairs.

Laurie was a little cautious, but also delighted at the pastor's enthusiasm. A month later, Laurie turned up to see 50 people wearing T-shirts that proudly declared that Jesus loved his school. They cleaned gutters, pulled weeds, painted the outside of classrooms, and picked up more rubbish than he thought possible. A team had coordinated lunch and he gladly accepted the invitation to join them. Tradespeople fixed tiles, repaired holes, replaced light bulbs, and managed to get stuck windows open. A photographer was busy all day.

By the end of the day, the school was transformed. Everyone sat in the school hall watching the before and after photos, cheering their own hard work.

On Monday morning, the students and teachers were stunned by how much had changed over the weekend. Laurie gave a heartfelt tribute to the church during school assembly, and the church and school continued to have a close relationship while Laurie was principal there.

This is at a time when Christianity is being forced out of most public schools in Australia. The privilege of teaching Scripture in schools is under threat, and there is even a move to prevent churches from holding services on school property (many schools let out facilities on Sundays).

I am sure that this example of service gave Christian teachers and parents involved with the school opportunity to promote or even explain the power of the gospel to transform not just individuals but communities.

A Christmas Party

I had a preaching engagement at a church, and during the announcements Louise stood up. She needed volunteers for the choir, and to serve at her work Christmas party.

Intrigued, I approached her after service and asked her to explain what she had organised. She described how she had joined the social committee of her organisation, a medium-player in the finance industry. There had been discussions about organising the annual Christmas party, and she had come up with an idea.

She had suggested holding the party in the company's boardroom, to keep the costs down, and recommended her church to perform Christmas songs and serve the food. The idea was warmly accepted, but there was one problem — she had not asked the church for permission!

Thankfully her pastor loved the idea. With his energetic support, a choir was organised, carols chosen, and enough volunteers gathered to help with the food. The songs gave an opportunity to gently explain the Christmas story, the reason for the celebration.

Louise's workmates were thrilled with the entertainment, and amazed that church members would give up their time to serve in that way. There was the opportunity for conversations about church, Jesus, faith; and for the pastor to learn more about Louise's workplace and colleagues.

Louise's pastor later told me that he doubted that many of her colleagues would ever have thought of coming to church, but in this astonishing case, the workplace invited the church to visit them!

Chaplaincy Based in the Local Church

In the last chapter, we examined the possibilities of chaplaincy and what it would mean if every Christian worker saw herself or himself as an informal chaplain in the workplace.

However, some churches have been quite deliberate about chaplaincy as a strategy. I met Steve who is a sports chaplain to the indoor cricket centre situated on the church property. His role is seen as entirely natural, and recently he presided at the first wedding from among the players. The church was full, and the bride and groom even staged a gentle game of indoor cricket down the aisle.

Mike is chaplain to the café that runs on his church property. He knows all the staff by the name, and they know he is available for prayer, counsel, and support. He has even managed to refer some of the staff to better-paid roles at other cafés and restaurants.

Petra has managed to convince many members of her congregation to be involved in emergency services chaplaincy. She has trained them up in critical incident response skills, and they are able to be mobilised quickly to respond to natural disasters.

Chaplaincy has been described as 'the church beyond the walls', and is most effective when done in conjunction with the local church, each supporting and building on each other.

Church in the Marketplace

Some churches are focused on helping the workers in their congregations to see their workplaces as mission fields, and others are looking at creative ways of connecting with workplaces. Some churches, though, have completely re-envisioned their concept of church and place, and actually relocated *into* the marketplace.

CrossLife is an example of such a church. There was a massive residential and commercial complex being planned for the fringe of a city, and the developer was interested in partnering with a church to provide community onsite. Most denominations did not like the developer's requirements.

CrossLife was in a neighbouring suburb and agreed to partner. The developer said that it wanted the church to be part of the process of building community, but it did not want the church to look like a church. The church could run the community centre and hold its services there on Sundays.

It was anticipated that the community centre would also house a café and a childcare centre. However, the church could not openly use those facilities to proselytise.

CrossLife took up the challenge that the other churches rejected, and it has been a stunning success. The pastor believes their church has a weekly connection with 450 families, the majority of whom they would otherwise not reach.

The church itself has 300 families involved, and is growing rapidly. Independent research was conducted to test the acceptance of the church's activities by the community. An amazing 97% of respondents agreed that it was at least somewhat appropriate that the church run the community centre. More than half, 53%, put the highest ranking, that it was absolutely appropriate for the church to run the centre.

Pastor Matt of CrossLife explained the difference of approach with two simple examples. After seeing the success of CrossLife's venture, another church is seeking to build a childcare centre on their church site. Matt points out that their priorities are back-to-front, "They want to plan for their kids' ministry and then build the childcare centre. They should build the childcare centre and put the kids' ministry in it."

A second example was the carols service which CrossLife ran. Instead of the church planning and running the activity, and inviting the community to come along, they asked the community what it wanted to do, then made the event possible.

"We need to see the church as the servant of the community, helping out and walking alongside them," Matt explains.

Business as Church

A more controversial model is when a business evolves to become a church. Jamie is one of the most inspiring Christians I know. He runs a gym that specialises in mixed martial arts.

Renegade is not just a gym. It is a place of community. First of all, Jamie has worked hard to break down the egocentric nature of most gyms. There are no mirrors — it is not a place where you put headphones on and work out on your own. The bathrooms are basic, rather than places to strut and preen.

Secondly, it is an inclusive community. When you ask about the fees, Jamie tells you to come and work out a few times, then pay what you think it is worth. This has enabled those who are struggling or marginalised to join the community, and work out alongside high-income doctors and businesspeople.

Thirdly, Jamie's focus is fitness, not beauty. He will work hard to help you reach your training goals, but it is the work that will be commended and celebrated, not the resultant body. People are also acknowledged for how much they help others as training partners, or even if they simply clean up around the gym.

It was obvious to me — and I told him so — that Jamie was a pastor and the gym members his congregation. He taught them, cared for them, loved them, and modelled Jesus to them. He regularly holds baptisms at beaches for those who have asked more about the man-God Jesus, whom they see motivates Jamie.

Recently, Jamie started up Renegade Church, monthly services at the gym. It is a risky move, but it may be the right time. Jamie has been to Bible college and earned his theology degree, and he preaches with heart. He is contextualising church for the people who come to the gym.

Other Ideas?
These are some of the ways the church is connecting with workplaces, but there is no end to the possibilities. All it takes is recognition that the workplace is a legitimate place for missional activity.

Prayer:

Thank you Lord,

For the ways you are opening up opportunities for the church in various workplaces.

For the willingness of your people to get involved.

For the riskiness of some of these moves.

For the great reward.

For the reality that the church gathered and scattered has a legitimate place at work.

For the work Jesus has done.

For the ongoing work of the Spirit.

For your work as creating, sustaining, redeeming, reconciling, and restoring all things.

AMEN

Taking It Further:

1

Make a note of all the businesses within a one-kilometre radius of your church. How could your church be a blessing to them? Walk past those businesses and pray for them. Ask God for opportunities to connect.

2

Check out Jamie Murray's work with Renegade Gym and Church. Type "Renegade MMA & BJJ" into YouTube. You will see baptisms, sermons, and interviews, as well as their work establishing gyms for underprivileged communities overseas. See if any of the principles described here could apply to your business or workplace.

3

Paul combined his work and his preaching and teaching. Read the following verses to get a sense of his link between the two: Acts 18:2–3; Acts 20:34–35; 1 Corinthians 9:12, 10:31; Colossians 3:23; 1 Thessalonians 2:9, 4:11–12; and 2 Thessalonians 3:6–13.

4

Review all the stories outlined in this chapter and choose at least one initiative that you will work on with your church. Think of a team of people who could work with you to make it a reality.

Appendix 1
Interview Preparation Guide

The following material comes from Matthew Waldron, pastor at the Three Crosses Church in Perth, Australia, and provides an excellent resource for churches interested in interviewing workplace Christians.[1] It consists of:

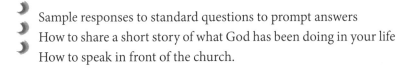

Sample responses to standard questions to prompt answers

How to share a short story of what God has been doing in your life

How to speak in front of the church.

Some of the material is based on the 6Ms from *Fruitfulness on the Frontline*.[2] More information on these can be found at the London Institute of Contemporary Christianity.[3]

This Time Tomorrow
Interviews at church to share about our day-to-day lives

Sometimes we have specific reasons to interviewing someone, because they are new or leaving, or have particular news to share. But we also just regularly want to get people up to share about their day-to-day life trusting Jesus. This document gives ideas about how to prepare encouraging answers to our standard questions, how to share a story about what God has been doing in your life, and how to actually stand up and do it! (If you're feeling nervous, you might be encouraged by 1 Corinthians 14:26)

Standard Questions
The questions are not set in stone, so feel free to suggest alternatives or additional ones. But our standard questions are:

---

[1] My thanks to Léni-Jo McMillan for making me aware of this resource and permission to use it.
[2] Mark Greene, *Fruitfulness on the Frontline* (Nottingham: InterVarsity Press, 2014).
[3] https://www.licc.org.uk/resources/discover-fruitfulness-on-the-frontline/ (cited 28-Feb-2018).

- What will you be doing this time tomorrow?
- What is a joy in that?
- What is a struggle in that?
- What (else) can we pray for you?

Standard Answers

One of the things we want to grow in together is living our whole lives for Jesus. So it is helpful as we prepare for the interview, and helpful for everyone when we share, if our answers point to Christ and his kingdom. Here are suggested ways we could do that for the standard set of questions.

1. What will you be doing this time tomorrow?
   - Start with the specifics of what you will be doing on the actual Monday morning in question. E.g. Laying bricks, meeting with a client, making follow-up phone calls, taking orders.
   - Then describe the bigger gist of what you do. E.g. Being a builder, salesperson, engineer, homemaker.
   - Then mention how this contributes to the world (without mentioning God yet).

2. What is a joy in that?
   - Pick one or two things. E.g. I like working with my hands, I like being creative, I like helping people.
   - Give a concrete example without oversharing. E.g. Last week, I installed a…/sold a…/helped a student…
   - Express thankfulness to God. E.g. I'm thankful to God for my role, I'm glad God has created me that way, I'm very blessed.

3. What is a struggle in that?
   - Pick one or two things. E.g. I hate working with my hands, I hate being creative, I hate helping people
   - Give a concrete example without oversharing. E.g. One time, I had to…/one of our clients…/a couple of my colleagues…

🌙 Express dependence on God. E.g. I'm praying that God will.../ I would love people to pray.../ I'm trusting God has a plan in that.

4. What (else) can we pray for you? This question can be skipped if you have already answered it to your satisfaction, or else add more items!

Sharing What God Has Been Doing in Your Life

It is great to share points of thanksgiving and prayer with one another. But it is also very helpful to share stories of what God has been doing in our lives. Sometimes, we can share how we became followers of Jesus. But there are lots of other things God is doing in our day-to-day lives as well! One of the things you can do in a church interview, though you don't need to, is share a story of something God has been doing in your life.

It builds up other Christians. It is a natural way of pointing to or sharing the gospel, and it is further opportunity to reflect and give thanks to God. It is also a correction for the secularism of our age, which discourages us from thinking, let alone talking, about God being active in our experience. You may think you have nothing worthwhile to share. But the Bible is full of ordinary people like us, impacted by the word of God, and producing a crop.

Here is a process you could work through to prepare a story of something God has been doing in your life.

What to Share

A story is usually prepared in this order: Fruit, Struggle, God, Context.

Fruit: What is one piece of fruit the gospel has produced in your life recently?

Brainstorm the following categories:

1. Modelling godly character — how have you been godly?
2. Making good work — how have you looked after the world and made it a good place?
3. Ministering grace and love — how have you treated people better than you had to?
4. Moulding culture — how have you influenced the way people do things in a positive direction?
5. (Being a) Mouthpiece for truth and justice — how have you spoken up for what is true or fair?
6. (Being a) Messenger of the Gospel — how have you shared the gospel?

Struggle: What is one thing that was difficult about that?
Brainstorm the following categories:

- Yourself
- Other people
- Circumstances

God: How did God relate to you in this situation?
Brainstorm the following categories:

- Bible: Encountering what God says in the Bible, reflecting on some doctrine, etc.
- People: Someone else saying or doing something.
- Wisdom: Thinking about things, figuring something out.
- Feelings: Feeling some emotion or desire.
- Nature: The glory of God displayed in the beauty, power, or coherence of creation.
- Circumstances: The reign of God displayed in the ordering of circumstances.

Context: What was your attitude to the promises of God regarding the situation beforehand?

It doesn't have to have changed but it may have. Briefly answer the following questions:

🌙 How did you understand God's promises regarding this situation?

🌙 How much did you call to mind God's promises?

🌙 How did you feel about God's promises?

How to Share
A story is usually told in this order: Context, Struggle, God, Fruit.

> *Context:* Put this in a nutshell for the person or people you are talking with.
>
> *Struggle:* Express this in terms of your experience without blaming or criticising.
>
> *God:* Decide whether to describe God's action in the active or passive voice. E.g. Say, "God convicted me I needed to act", or "I felt convicted I needed to act".
>
> *Fruit:* Describe briefly for the person or people you are talking with.

It is often good to finish with one sentence on the difference the experience has made — or what you hope it might make — to you or someone else.

Fitting a Story into an Interview
Once you have figured out a story to share, you can decide whether it fittingly answers one of the existing questions or whether it needs another question. If a new question is added, it can be structured very broadly, such as, "In the midst of all that struggle going on, how have you seen God at work in your life?"; or very narrowly, "You were telling me something really encouraging happened this week with one of your friends?"

Speaking in Front of the Church

Here are three suggestions to make speaking in front of the church (or any group of people) enjoyable for you and the people listening!

1. Use notes in point form

   There may be occasions when you don't need notes, or when you want to write down every word you wish to say. However, as a general rule for most people speaking their first language — if you need full notes, it may be too complicated!

2. Practise

   What kind of and how much of practice is up to you to negotiate between your nerves and your busy life. But anything you haven't done before is worth practicing, such as using the microphone, being interviewed, projecting your voice, or putting your notes into full sentences.

3. Relax, smile, and look

   When you stand up the front to speak, relax, smile, and look where you are supposed to be looking. As a good start, face the front. In an interview, whoever is not speaking should be looking at the person who is. The speaker should either be looking at the people in the congregation, or if that is too confronting, just over the heads of the people in the back row.

Appendix 2
Mentoring Program[1]

In Chapter 18, we established the importance of mentoring and discipling workplace Christians. Although good statistics are difficult to find, it is sufficiently clear that there is a huge falling away from faith during the first couple of years of working.[2] All the hard work and resources that we put into children's, youth, and university ministries may be squandered.

There is also the need to affirm people in their working as a means of worshiping God. It enables people to be more productive, to flourish in both their working and their faith.

In response to requests, I have drawn up the following mentoring program, based on the spiritual disciplines described in *Workship* Volume 1, Section 2. There is more detail in those chapters, but the following may be easier to run in six one-hour sessions.

Introduction

Welcome to this mentoring program, which will look at gospel expression at work. It will take in all aspects of the gospel — the good news that Jesus has come and has a mission of redemption, not just personally, but for all the places where sin has its grip. We are talking about both **proclamation** and **practice** of the gospel message of reconciliation and transformation.

You will learn six ways that the gospel can be expressed, referred to as spiritual disciplines for working (Note: they are **not** mutually exclusive). A spiritual discipline is a habit, or a way of looking, which needs to be practised and which illuminates an element of God's truth and/or brings the believer closer to God.

---

[1] I would like to thank Patrick Chua for the inspiration to write this Appendix, with his wonderful heart for discipling, and his desire to make it simple to mentor workplace Christians.

[2] In the UK, only 11% of regular churchgoers are between the ages of 25 and 34 (http://www.christian-research.org/uploads/quadrant/backcopies/Quad362013.pdf cited 30-Dec-2017). In Australia, it is 10%, and represents the biggest gap between population size and attendance (Source: NCLS Occasional Paper 19, May 2013).

Here are the six spiritual disciplines identified in this program.

- **Holy Working** — for those with a focus on virtue, who see work as training in godliness, who are wary about temptations in the workplace, who work hard and well, and who value moral purity.
- **Gospel Working** — for those who are keen to evangelise where appropriate, promote the truth in their workplace, focus on obedience, and enjoy running Bible studies, gospel discovery series (such as *Alpha*), and prayer meetings or support groups.
- **Prayerful Working** — for those who particularly value prayer and reflection, who focus on their relationship with God while working, who see the Christian life as lived out in the midst of the everyday.
- **Incarnational Working** — for those who see their work as partnering with God in his work, as being God's hands and feet, who look for symbols of God's presence, who seek to make God visible through what they do.
- **Spirit-Empowered Working** — for those who are spiritually gifted, who experience God's empowering in their work, who seek to transform their workplace and look for opportunities to bless others through their working.
- **Social Justice Working** — for those who are compassionate and love justice, who look for opportunities for mercy at work, who seek fair treatment for all, and who are passionate about their work.

These six frames were developed using the Renovaré balanced vision of life with Christ: contemplative, holiness, charismatic, social justice, evangelical, and incarnational.[3]

---

[3] "The Six Streams: A Balanced Vision", *Renovaré*. https://renovare.org/about/ideas/the-six-streams (cited 28-Feb-2018).

Session 1

Holy Working

We can use our spiritual muscles to improve the way we approach our work. Some people call these spiritual disciplines. It means we actually apply ourselves to habits that can improve our working.

Holy Working is virtuous, with a focus on personal moral transformation and training in godliness. It emphasizes a deeply moral life, purity, a way of living which stands out from the world. There is a focus on sanctification, that we are being transformed into the people we were meant to be, and that the fruit of our lives might bear the fruit of the spirit (Galatians 5:22–23): love, joy, peace, patience, kindness, goodness, faithfulness, gentleness and self control.

In many ways, work is the perfect context to develop such fruit. It is where we are often most tested in terms of our patience, gentleness, faithfulness to God and self-control. We should be praying for ways to express love, make peace, celebrate joy, be kind, and do good.

Reflection at work

- What are some of the temptations in your workplace, which distract you from Holy Working?
- Read Galatians 5:22–23. Which characteristic of the fruit of the Spirit do you most need to work on in the workplace?

What does the Bible say?

Focusing on just one aspect of the fruit — love — think about how the following verses apply to your workplace:

> Love is patient, love is kind. It does not envy, it does not boast, it is not proud. It does not dishonor others, it is not self-seeking, it is not easily angered, it keeps no record of wrongs. Love does not delight in evil but rejoices with the truth. It always protects, always trusts, always hopes, always perseveres (1 Corinthians 13:4–7).

It is often tougher to express love appropriately in the workplace, but easier to think of times when we need to be patient or to show kindness. We can ensure that we do not boast of our achievements, focusing on empowering others rather than ourselves. We can ensure we honour others, seek the good for others, do not lose our tempers, and are gracious. We can seek out ways to hold back evil and promote truth. We can protect our colleagues and customers, build up trust, encourage others to hope, and persevere under pressure.

Mentoring question

> What is the challenge to you of working in this way? How can your mentor pray for you?

Prayer

Dear Lord,

We know that in our working we are often tempted to live lives that are not marked by holiness or purity. Please help us to hold fast to your truth, to be challenged to live lives at work that look different, sound different, and influence others positively.

Help us not to lower our standards at work. Rather, help us to be known as people who demonstrate what it means to show love, express joy, bring peace, demonstrate patience, be kind, do good to others, be faithful to the example of Jesus, display gentleness, and show self-control.

May we have people who can hold us accountable, who can pray through the difficult choices we may have to make, and who can celebrate with us when we are able to make a stand for truth, beauty, justice, and what is good.

Amen

Session 2

Gospel Working

We can use our spiritual muscles to improve the way we approach our work. Some people call these spiritual disciplines. It means we actually apply ourselves to habits that can improve our working. Last time we met, we looked at Holy Working.

Gospel Working is Bible-centred, and focuses on the proclamation of the good news of the gospel either lived or spoken. It emphasises sharing faith, encountering Christ in Scripture, living the Christ-life, exercising a Bible-shaped working, and speaking the truth in love.

In practising this spiritual discipline, there are some simple behaviours we can demonstrate in the workplace:

- Focus on living and working obediently.
- Look to integrate biblical knowledge with working.
- Defend the truth.
- Link up with other Christians, forming a Bible study, gospel discovery group, prayer meetings, or support groups.
- Seek every opportunity to bear witness to the gospel in work and deed.

Reflection at work

- How can you apply more of your biblical knowledge in your working, and/or responding to fellow workers? What do you need to do to make that happen?
- It is going to be increasingly difficult to identify as a Christian in our workplaces. What are some legitimate ways you can be open about your faith?

What does the Bible say?

Gospel Working is inspired by Jesus' call to be salt and light (the inspiration for the organisation that compiles these devotions for you):

You are the salt of the earth. But if the salt loses its saltiness, how can it be made salty again? It is no longer good for anything, except to be thrown out and trampled underfoot. You are the light of the world. A town built on a hill cannot be hidden. Neither do people light a lamp and put it under a bowl. Instead they put it on its stand, and it gives light to everyone in the house. In the same way, let your light shine before others, that they may see your good deeds and glorify your Father in heaven. (Matthew 5:13–16)

Jesus is challenging us about the way we work, our behaviour, and our speaking — that people might see our distinctiveness as Christians, and our good deeds, and be moved to glorify the God who motivates us.

We need to be particularly careful in how we share the Word of God. The danger is that we might distort the Bible's message to benefit ourselves, or to suit our audience (2 Corinthians 4:2). In this passage, Paul points out to the Corinthians that the people around us are blinded to gospel truth, but we must be careful to preach Jesus and not ourselves. We need to make sure that we do not manipulate what the Bible says to make ourselves look good, or to avoid difficult truth, or to simply make a point in an argument, which may be a temptation in the workplace. Instead we should serve those we work with, in accordance with the truth and wisdom of the Scriptures, as part of our obedience to God (Ephesians 6:5–9).

Mentoring question
- In what ways are you salt and light in your workplace?
- Read Ephesians 6:5–9. How do these verses challenge you in your working?

Prayer
Loving God,
Thank you for the gift of your Word that informs not just what we

believe, but how we act. Help us to be careful in the way we use the Bible in the workplace — to be faithful to its message, and in ways that help us live at peace, but which remains faithful to what it says.

Help us to be like Jesus, who used working situations to teach great truths. Help us to make links between our working and your Word. Help us to be conscious of those who have particular need for the wisdom of the Scriptures. Help us to have opportunity to clarify and explain what your Word says.

Grant us courage to take every opportunity to reveal the good news of new life in Jesus, whether through words, organising activities, or specific good deeds — but especially in the way we work and what we accomplish with our working.

Amen

Session 3
Prayerful Working

We can use our spiritual muscles to improve the way we approach our work. Some people call these spiritual disciplines. It means we actually apply ourselves to habits that can improve our working. In this mentoring series, we have already looked at Holy Working and Gospel Working.

Prayerful Working emphasises spiritual reflection and continuous prayer. People who cultivate this way of working have a calm ability to be still in the midst of busyness, and are often very contemplative in their approach to issues. There is a spiritual depth to their conversation, and they have often developed the discipline of Christian meditation.

In practising this spiritual discipline, there are some simple behaviours we can demonstrate in the workplace:

- An awareness of God's presence.
- The ability to bring everything before God either openly or internally.
- Being able to create rhythms of rest, silence, and even solitude in the work environment. While this may be much easier with routine jobs, or roles that involve contact with the natural environment, it can be done anywhere and anytime with some creativity.
- Demonstrate the celebration of the good things of God: achievements, truth, goodness, beauty, wonder, and joy.
- Honouring the holy days of the church calendar.

Reflection at work

- How prayerful are you about your working? Who can you meet up with to pray about your work?
- How can you pray more deliberately for your organisation? What are the things that need to change to give it more of the fragrance of the kingdom, and the blessings of God that you see in the work and/or relationships?

What does the Bible say?

We need hearts, minds, and spirits that are open to seeing God's fingerprints in what happens around us and what is done through us. Unfortunately, many interpret this awareness of God as requiring that we leave the noise and bustle of the everyday life.

While occasional retreats should be encouraged, we cannot depend on that, especially in our working days. The spirituality of withdrawal movement often quotes Psalm 46:10: "Be still and know that I am God." However, the irony of that verse being used in that way, is that the context of Psalm 46 is the busyness of the city, and circumstances that are far from tranquil. The psalmist feels earthquakes and tidal waves. Nations are in uproar and kingdoms are falling. In spite of this, the psalmist finds the way to be still, that he might know God.

In our chaotic and crazy lives, where being busy is a status symbol, we need to be reminded that peace is a sign of God's presence. God says clearly in Isaiah 30:15 that, "In repentance and rest is your salvation, in quietness and trust is your strength". This is in contrast to the constant striving that characterises modern life.

Mentoring question

❯ How will you commit to pray through the day, even in the mess, chaos, and busyness?

❯ Write out a specific prayer for some of the challenges or opportunities you are facing in your workplace right now. Commit to praying that prayer every morning for a week. Journal any answers to prayer, any unexpected opportunities, any blessings on your working, any disappointments.

Prayer

Our Lord,

So often we are distracted while we work by our busyness, concerns or frustrations. So often we are consumed by our own thoughts and actions, rather than being aware of your presence. Rarely do we consider our work in light of your sovereignty and power.

We want to set this right. So we ask that for every moment of our working this day, we might be conscious of your presence with us — of your work around us, in us, and through us.

We ask that we might contemplate and evaluate our work in the light of our worship of you. We ask that we might rededicate ourselves to serving you through our work.

Before we start work, incline us to welcome you into our work through prayer. Regularly as we work, help us to involve and seek you through prayer. As we finish our working, help us to be grateful for the opportunity and privilege of working with you.

Amen

Session 4
Incarnational Working

We can use our spiritual muscles to improve the way we approach our work. Some people call these spiritual disciplines. It means we actually apply ourselves to habits that can improve our working. In this mentoring series we have already looked at Holy Working, Gospel Working, and Prayer Working.

Incarnational Working is about making God visible to those around us, and bearing witness to God at work in the world, in us, through us, and (often) in spite of us. Its emphasis is on everyday sacraments, and seeing God alive in symbols and metaphors.

In practising this spiritual discipline, there are some simple behaviours we can demonstrate in the workplace:

- An awareness of symbols of God's presence.
- The ability to discern metaphors of creation, faithfulness, redemption, salvation, provision, and grace.
- Living like Jesus and doing what he would do, especially in serving those around us.
- The capacity to see our work as the source material for modern parables to pass on God's wisdom and the gospel.

Reflection at work
- How easy is it to practise the discipline of Incarnational Working in your workplace? What are the challenges and opportunities?
- How can you proclaim as well as promote an awareness of God's goodness and grace?

What does the Bible say?
It is clear that the visible creation is evidence of the master designer-creator, and we bear witness to God when we acknowledge the wonder of his creation. "The heavens declare the glory of God; the skies proclaim the work of his hands," says Psalm 19:1.

Just as Jesus was God made visible ("The Word became flesh and made his dwelling among us. We have seen his glory, the glory of the one and only Son, who came from the Father, full of grace and truth." — John 1:14), we make God visible to those around us in the way we work, how we behave, and what we do.

In John 5:17, Jesus says that God is still working, which must mean he works through people and their speech and activities. We can cooperate with God at work, and turn our work into an act of worship. Colossians 1:15–17 tells us that since his ascension Jesus is sovereign over all creation and "in him all things hold together." Our work becomes an opportunity to acknowledge his lordship.

Mentoring question

- In what ways can you be the visible expression of the Trinity: Father, Jesus, and the Spirit, at your work?
- How can the way you work and the outcome of your work be an expression of your worship of God?

Prayer

Dear God,

We are excited and frightened by the possibility of being your eyes and ears, hands and feet in the world. It is a great privilege to make you more visible to the people around us. It is also a great responsibility.

Help us to stay in tune with you in our working, that we might faithfully continue your work in this world. Help us to be conscious of how we might bear witness to your character through our work; and how we might continue your great work of creating, redeeming, bringing justice, caring, sustaining, and providing.

Thank you for the wonderful example of Jesus.

Amen

Session 5
Spirit-Empowered Working

We have been looking at how we can use our spiritual muscles to improve the way we approach our work. Some people call these spiritual disciplines. It means we actually apply ourselves to habits that can improve our working. In this mentoring series we have already looked at Holy Working, Gospel Working, Prayer Working, Incarnational Working.

Spirit-Empowered Working is focused on using the spiritual gifts in the workplace, and seeing our work as a place where God can work miraculously. It is an acknowledgement that God's presence is everywhere by his Spirit, even in seemingly unlikely places.

It is also recognition that God makes his power available to us by his Spirit. As Paul told Timothy, "For this reason I remind you to fan into flame the gift of God, which is in you through the laying on of my hands. For the Spirit God gave us does not make us timid, but gives us power, love and self-discipline" (2 Timothy 1:6–7).

In practising this spiritual discipline, there are some simple behaviours we can demonstrate in the workplace:

-) Discover your spiritual gifts, and seek wisdom on how to develop and use them.
-) Pray for opportunities to partner with God in what he is already doing in the workplace.
-) Welcome God's presence.
-) Seek to serve those you work with to enhance the workplace environment.

Reflection at work
-) How comfortable are you with the notion of God working through you by his Spirit in your workplace? What encouragement do you receive from this chapter? What challenges you?
-) What spiritual gifts do you believe you have been given? What are

some ways you might be able to exercise them in the workplace or in your working?

What does the Bible say?

I love the story of Bezalel from Exodus 31:1–5:

> *Then the Lord said to Moses, 'See I have chosen Bezalel son of Uri, the son of Hur, of the tribe of Judah, and I have filled him with the Spirit of God, with wisdom, with understanding, with knowledge and with all kinds of skills – to make artistic designs for work in gold, silver and bronze, to cut and set stones, to work in wood, and to engage in all kinds of crafts.*

Bezalel is a reminder that God equips us for the work we are to do. In this case, it was to design the Tent of Meeting for the Israelites in the desert.

Although this is a specific pouring out of God's Spirit, it is clear that God prepares work for us to do: "For we are God's handiwork, created in Christ Jesus to do good works, which God prepared in advance for us to do" (Ephesians 2:10). He also equips us to do it, as the writer to the Hebrews reminds us, "Now may the God of peace, who through the blood of the eternal covenant brought back from the dead our Lord Jesus, that great Shepherd of the sheep, equip you with everything good for doing his will, and may he work in us what is pleasing to him, through Jesus Christ, to whom be glory for ever and ever. Amen" (Hebrews 13:20–21).

1 Corinthians 12:7 tells us that these gifts are given for the common good of all his creation: "Now to each one the manifestation of the Spirit is given for the common good."

Mentoring question

- ❯ What are some of the special gifts God has given you for your working?
- ❯ How has God equipped you to do your work?

🌙 How can you be more open with others about the way God has both gifted and equipped you?

Prayer
God of power,

Thank you for the gift of your Spirit who enables us to do so much more than we might in our own strength.

Help us to increasingly work in step with the Spirit, aware of promptings to speak or act. Help us to be more aware of how you enable us for the work that you have provided.

Let us not be shy in using the gifts you have given us by your Spirit, especially for the common good. As we see you powerfully at work, help us remember that it is for your glory and not our own.

Amen

Session 6

Social Justice Working

Here is our last spiritual discipline in this mentoring series. We have been looking at how we can use our spiritual muscles to improve the way we approach our work. We have been applying ourselves to habits that can improve our working. We have already looked at Holy Working, Gospel Working, Prayer Working, Incarnational Working, and Spirit-Empowered Working.

Social Justice Working is an expression of compassion, focusing on bringing God's justice to bear on work activities. It is also an expression of *shalom*, a word often weakly translated as 'peace' but which means so much more. It is about bringing about completeness, wholeness, wellbeing and harmony. Social Justice Working means that you focus on the way things could and should be — the way things would be in all their fullness. This especially relates to working relationships and work structures.

In practising this spiritual discipline, there are some simple behaviours we can demonstrate in the workplace:

- Strive for workplace reform to ease the burden on vulnerable workers, consumers, or suppliers.
- Agitate for equal opportunity.
- Seek to express compassion in the workplace.

Reflection at work

- What areas of your working have practices that might be considered unjust? Are there areas of inequity you have been inspired to act or speak up against?
- How can you develop the discipline of Social Justice in your working? Is there a group who are vulnerable that you can advocate for, or a way of introducing more compassionate practices?

What does the Bible say?

Many Christians interested in justice know Micah 6:8 well, where the Lord explains that he is not as pleased by sacrifices, as by those who "act justly and to love mercy and to walk humbly with your God." The rest of the passage describes some of the unjust work practices that displease God, including ill-gotten treasures, dishonest scales, false weights, and deceitful talk.

This theme of workplace practices criticised by God continues in Habakkuk 2:6–20. The passage here includes stolen goods, extortion, unjust gain, waste of people's labour, anything which impoverishes or causes violence to others, exploitation of people for gratification, and idolising of anything other than God.

Social Justice Working takes up the call of Habakkuk to bring justice and thus fill the earth "with the knowledge of the glory of the Lord as the waters cover the sea" (verse 14).

We see Jesus' concern for justice in his anger against the Pharisees for leading believers astray and for their hypocritical behaviour (Matthew 23). Most publicly, he overturned the tables at the Temple, aggravated by the way women and gentiles have had their worship space occupied by those who seek to profit from the poor (Matthew 21:12–17).

In Acts 22:22–29, Paul used the law to his advantage when he claimed his rights as a Roman citizen to avoid being whipped and receive a trial. Our astute understanding of government rules and regulations will allow us to maximise our effectiveness as Christians, although our priority should be on easing the burdens on others, as Paul did when he returned Onesimus, the runaway slave, to his owner, advocating on his behalf (see Philemon).

Mentoring question

> How can you use your influence at work to ease the burdens of others: fellow workers, customers, and/or suppliers?

◗ What long-term justice project can you begin praying about: a deep ethical issue, a transformation of work practice, or a change in product?

Prayer
Lord of justice and truth,

We are conscious of your passion for justice, truth, peace, and wholeness. Help us to see ways we can weave justice into our activities at work.

Help us to be conscious of the ways our working might be exploitive, harmful, or unfair, and to have the courage to change what we can. Help us to see the way work structures can perpetuate inequity, discrimination, and hurt, and to have the courage to change what we can.

Help us to see our workplace and our colleagues through your eyes of compassion. Give us energy, enthusiasm, and persistence to fight for your justice.

Amen

Acknowledgements

I want to start by acknowledging God: for inviting me to work with him, and for using my passion for writing. May every word in this book bring him glory. I am enthused by Jesus' living, working, and sacrifice, and the Spirit's prompting and advocacy.

I am thankful to David, Jaslyn, and Guy for your patience and belief in me, and your willingness to free me up to travel and speak.

Thank you to my friends, especially An-Magritt who continues to read me and provide wisdom and insight. Thank you also to my prayer partners: Isabel, Jill, Christine, Cathy; and Diane, Nadja, and Karen.

Thank you to my publisher Graceworks for risking Volume 2; and Charmain for being willing to labour through my text, making me sound better than I am.

Thank you to all the people whose stories appear in this book. I hope that your stories will enable others to find themselves in God's grand story of working with us to care for this world, with glimpses of the New Creation.

Thank you to every church that has invited me to preach, or asked me to partner them in their faith and work initiatives. Thank you for every invitation to speak or present a workshop. I am grateful also to those who have liked my Facebook page, followed my website, and sent ideas and encouragement.

For those who are **struggling** at work: be of good courage, you are God's workmanship and he has created good work for you to do.

For those who **love** their work: keep honouring God and serving others through your working, remembering that you are partnering God in his work.

For those who are wondering if they have found their true **vocation**: keep asking God to help you find your identity in Christ, that he may work through your passions, gifts, skills, concerns, and experiences.

For those who have **finished** their paid work: may God continue to establish the work of your hands and lead you to new opportunities to glorify him in whatever you do.